Our Paris

for Shirley
all my best

Ed White

Our Paris

SKETCHES FROM MEMORY

Edmund White
with Drawings by Hubert Sorin

ecco
An Imprint of HarperCollinsPublishers

HarperCollins books may be purchased for educational, business, or sales promotional use. For information please write: Special Markets Department, HarperCollins Publishers Inc., 10 East 53rd Street, New York, NY 10022.

First published in the United States by Alfred A. Knopf, Inc., in 1994. Originally published in Great Britain as *Sketches from Memory: People and Places in the Heart of Our Paris* by Chatto & Windus and Picador in 1994.

Designed by Sarah Maya Gubkin

Library of Congress Cataloging-in-Publication Data
  White, Edmund, 1940-
  [Sketches from memory]
    Our Paris : sketches from memory / Edmund White and [with draw-ings by] Hubert Sorin—1st ed.
       p.   cm.
    Originally published under the title: Sketches from memory.
  London : Chatto & Windus : Picador, 1994. Reprinted under the title:
  Our Paris. New York : Knopf, 1995. ISBN 0-06-008592-4 (hardcover)
    1. 4e Arrondissement (Paris, France)—Social life and
  customs—Pictorial works. 2. Paris(France)—Social life and
  customs—20th century. 3. White, Edmund, 1940—Homes and
  haunts—France—Paris. 4. Americans—France—Paris—History—20th century. 5. Sorin, Hubert—Homes and haunts—France—Paris. 6. Gay
  men—France—Paris—Biography. 7. AIDS (Disease)—France—Paris.
  I.Sorin, Hubert. II. Title.
  DC752.A04 W48 2002   2001051268

02 03 04 05 06 ❖/ QBM 10 9 8 7 6 5 4 3 2 1

To Julien Sorin

OUR PARIS:
A NEW INTRODUCTION

by Edmund White

UNLIKE AMERICAN CITIES, which change completely
right under our eyes and can go through two or three
total transformations in the course of a lifetime, the
great European cities look the same as they did in photos taken a hundred years ago. Maybe the benches and
kiosks are of a new design—or have been newly
designed to resemble an earlier look—and maybe the
gas lamps are now electrified, but the layout of the
squares and the appearance of the statues and fountains
and palaces are eternal. In old photos, of course, the
women are wearing long dresses and shawls and the

men have floppy ties or top hats, which makes it all the stranger to see them mounted on the same stage as we are.

Paris is, of course, in constant flux. Before 1850 it was a smelly, cramped, chaotic, medieval collection of villages; after 1870 and the changes wrought by Napoleon III and his master builder, the Baron Haussmann, it was a modern city. Everything in Paris—from the twelve avenues radiating out from the Arc de Triomphe to the graceful layout of the new Bois de Boulogne with its two artificial lakes, from the innovative design of the glass and metal stalls of the food markets at Les Halles to the botched transformation of the Île de la Cité from a dangerous but picturesque medieval slum to an arid administrative center—everything was thought out and calculated down to the tiniest detail by the tall Alsatian workaholic, Haussmann, the Prefect of the Seine.

In the years I lived in Paris President Mitterand, infected with the true French *folie de grandeur*, had also rebuilt Paris, starting with its most important axis. He'd placed I. M. Pei's glass pyramid in the courtyard of the Louvre and, at the other end of the axis, beyond the prancing horses of Marly on the Place de la Concorde and beyond the Arc de Triomphe, he'd erected a brand new arch—a massive square in stone that crowns the city of modern offices, the Champs-Elysées was widened and outfitted with new "park furniture," old neon was stripped away, even the paving stones were replaced.

In spite of all these changes, the city with its awnings and cafés, its broad avenues and plane trees, its uniform facades of apartment buildings and its great monuments (the Eiffel Tower, Notre Dame, the onion dome of Sacre Coeur above the hillside of Montmartre) all remain the same. This enduring look of Paris makes the changes in the lives of its citizens all the more poignant—the births and deaths, the illnesses and sudden removals.

When I wrote this little book I was living in the midst of huge personal changes that were almost mocked by the static solidity of the city around me. Hubert Sorin, the young French architect with whom I'd been living for five years, was dying of AIDS. When he had no longer been able to work, three years before he died, he had begun to develop his unique, exuberant drawing style, which was always, even from the first, linked to narration. He loved to tell stories about the people we were meeting and the places we were going. He had a sharp, satirical eye for pomposity and a loving, gentle, somehow compensating vision of frailty. We lived in Providence, Rhode Island, for a short spell while I taught at Brown, and Hubert was amused and fascinated by every cultural difference he observed (and there were many!). Back in Paris we attended many art openings and evening parties and little dinners and met people in politics, the art world, and publishing as well as the usual Parisian cast of the leisured unemployed. In every case Hubert was taking visual and verbal notes and working up comic strips about the events.

I remember one comic about the "great" Albanian writer Ismail Kadare. Everyone in our group went up to the novelist to be introduced and to coo with admiration, though in the end it came out that none of us had ever read a word by him. All this was taking place during an opening at the gallery that Rachel Stella (daughter of painter Frank Stella) was then running in the sixteenth arrondissement.

Hubert had a way of imagining that everything in our lives had a mythic resonance and would be instantly impressive to any reader or viewer, as if we were movie stars. I suppose that at a certain point I decided that if his delightful illustrations were ever going to be published (and that was his fondest hope, his dying wish), then I needed to temper the biting quality of his satire, which had become all the sharper as he was forced to contemplate an early death, and to tell the story of our local characters rather than of the very minor celebrities we were meeting. In the last weeks of his life I would stay up late writing down the brief chapters of this book and he would turn them into pictures.

Now Hubert is gone, Rachel Stella has moved to the

South of France, our concierge's son is dead (from alcoholism), she has retired to an old age home, the restaurant downstairs from us has closed for business, I live in New York—and the fairy tale of our life together, which was already somewhat heightened in the telling, now seems as insubstantial as a dream, though the setting, Paris, remains damnably eternal.

Our Paris

CHAPTER I

We were lying in bed one evening after dinner, digesting, idle as ever, the windows thrown wide open on the pulsing sky. Birds were wheeling above St.-Merri, and the pigeons, huddling between the geranium pots, were cooing (*roucoulement*, the French word, gives a better sense of the deep-throated, glottal contentment of the sound).

Hubert, as usual, was complaining about someone or something, and I said, "When you die and go to heaven you'll complain that your cloud isn't as *sympathique* as the next one." Fred was lying on his couch, chin on crossed paws, one eye cocked open and trained on us; he was wondering why we were already in bed when he hadn't had his late-night walk and it was still light out.

Like an orchestra tuning up before the conductor sweeps onto the podium and the curtain hisses up on the milling crowds for *La Bohème*, act 2, the restaurants downstairs were welcoming their first clients. A few glasses were tinkling and cutlery was chiming on china. A few people were laughing and a constant hum emitted by strollers was rising up to our fifth-floor windows.

"What a peaceful night," Hubert whispered. The sheets were clean, because we'd changed them that morning, and we felt as though we were drugged and melting into them. We must have fallen asleep for a moment, since when we awoke the sky was six shades closer to black and the restaurants' lights glowed from below like the gleam off the Rhine Maidens' sunken gold.

What woke us was a street singer's strong, even strident, voice accompanied by sketchy chords on an accordion and half-hearted strumming on a sadly out-of-tune guitar. The instruments may have been feeble but the singer's voice rang off the old walls in the narrow rue des Lombards with a sharp, ricocheting force.

"What's she singing?" I asked Hubert in the dark. I could barely see him. Usually he's hopeless about pop culture, as though he'd spent his entire youth in Ethiopia instead of just two years after architecture school, when, instead of serving in the army, he was sent by the French government to teach in Addis Ababa. But for once he surprised me and said, "It's Régine; it's so pretty, all about paper, crumpled paper, cardboard . . ." He can't really sing but he can hit the odd note with frightening operatic force, and now he let fly with one baritone shout that caused Fred to sigh in bored disapproval, though he thought the quickening signs of life looked promising for his walk.

"What do you think she looks like?" I asked.

"I was wondering exactly the same thing. She sounds to me very sophisticated," a word he uses in the older sense of "unnecessarily complicated," even "affected." "I think she's like Régine herself, red-haired, rather *forte* but not fat, backless spiked heels, hair swept up in a *brioche*, a *look sympa*. Someone with a rich, messy life."

As always his description surprised me and made me feel I didn't really know him. Anyway, his taste in women invariably strikes me as odd. He likes pale, sickly women with too much makeup, carefully applied, and expensive, impractical clothes; he has a horror of suntanned, natural, athletic American women.

"And you?" he asked.

"I see her as a peasant woman, short, wide, badly dressed, bronze hair curling with sweat and sticking to her big red face, a space between every tooth, thirty years old."

Hubert went to the window. Fred accompanied him, just to put in one more bid for his evening *sortie*. The song was over and Hubert joined in the applause.

"She's looking up," he said. "You know, it's fantastic. Your description is exactly right. I would never have guessed. Now I can see why you're such a good writer."

I was so idiotically pleased with this stroke of good descriptive luck that suddenly I wanted to go down and see my character at closer quarters. Fred was not reluctant to join me.

CHAPTER II

Hubert, like all Frenchmen, takes food very seriously and likes it fresh, so I go shopping every day on the rue Rambuteau, in the shadow of the Centre Georges Pompidou. This street runs through the no-man's-land between Les Halles (a faceless, modern shopping district, much of it below ground) and the upscale area of the Marais, the heart of aristocratic Paris in the seventeenth century and now the closest thing to a gay ghetto to be found in France. Despite the chic museum landmark, Rambuteau couldn't be more typically French (France, don't forget, is a country where the people spend a quarter of their income on food). There *is* a small supermarket, but since

I'm always with Fred and he's not welcome, I avoid it. All the other stores either open onto the street or are actually in it, like the little old flower man with his cart.

First Fred and I go to the fish man, who drives me mad because he insists on speaking English. Not that he knows anything *useful* in English, such as the names of fish or pounds instead of kilos. In a weak moment he once confessed to me that he hates the English (that was after he found out I was American), but then when the trade talks were going badly with the Americans and irate French fishermen were throwing their catch back in the ocean just to spite everyone, he announced he hated Americans, too, and was boycotting Euro Disney. He preferred to take his kids to something educational, such as that theme park outside Paris devoted entirely to scale models of important French châteaux. Not my idea of a fun family outing, but the French can't enjoy themselves if they don't think they're learning something. Ever notice how they crowd in front of the long, written explanations at the beginning of a museum show and whiz past the paintings themselves?

But he does have nice fish, and in the best French didactic manner he'll even write out recipes for me if I ask him. There he reverts to his native language and uses lovely expressions such as "a tear of wine" (*une larme de vin*), "a suspicion of ginger" (*un soupçon de gingembre*), "a cloud of milk" (*un nuage de lait*) or "a

nut of butter" (*une noix de beurre*). The best recipe he gave me was for mussels: "Brown two chopped onions and a piece of garlic in a thread of butter, then when they're transparent add two cups of dry white wine and a cup of water, salt and pepper, and a bay leaf. Let them bubble nicely while you clean a quart of mussels for each person. With your fingers pull off the beard (it rips off easily if you're pulling in the right direction). Throw away the mussels that are open when uncooked. Now put the good mussels in a casserole, cover with a lid, after five minutes shake them well to change their position and in five more minutes lift them out with a slotted spoon onto a waiting dish with a cover and pour the juice through a strainer lined with cheesecloth to remove the remaining grains of sand. Serve with a baguette for a hearty first course."

All in all Fred prefers the butcher, who is fat and red-faced, with an attractive scar that runs from chin to temple, and wears a dubiously bloody apron. He always remembers to give Fred a big bone. Fred gazes at him admiringly as he cuts the fat off steak, chops off a chicken's head, digs out the giblets, sews up the cavity and passes the trussed bird under the blowtorch to remove the last feathers. The word for "torch" is the most beautiful in French, *chalumeau*, a close rival to Edgar Allan Poe's proposal for the most beautiful sound in English, *cellar door*.

The fruit and vegetable man is young and handsome and an incorrigible skirt-chaser. If an attractive woman comes to his stall he tells his downtrodden assistant, "I'll take this one." Of course it would be sacrilege to palpate or even touch any of his produce; he's always shouting at Americans who can't read the warning sign—naturally, since it's written in French. His prices and stormy temperament are worth it, however, given that he can tell by smell alone the exact degree of ripeness for a melon, never sells rotting raspberries or fungusy blueberries, has eight kinds of lettuce, crisp tarragon, heavily perfumed basil, the subtlest chervil and even courgette flowers for deep-frying.

The cheese store smells either intriguing or repulsive, depending on your mood or health. There are so many cheeses—little "turds" (*crottins*) of goat cheese, runny Brie made from yummy unpasteurized milk, nightmarish rotting pyramids wrapped in leaves that remind you of nothing so much as vomit, even divinely bland cottage cheese made specially for the local Americans. I'm always reminded of de Gaulle's remark that it's impossible to rule a country that makes two hundred fifty kinds of cheese.

The Italian shop (the Casa di Pasta), the bakery with its irritating dog which always mounts a chagrined Fred, the wine store—at last we're heading home. Since I invariably forget my carryall, my hands are turning

9

red, cut and strangled by dozens of little blue plastic bags biting into them, and Fred is now fully awake, excited by the smell of the upcoming bone, and pulling feverishly every which way.

And to think my publisher wonders how I spend my days.

CHAPTER III

One of our neighbors is the famous couturier Azzedine Alaïa, the minuscule "architect of the body," as he's often called, because he creates his garments directly on his models. Whereas someone like Christian Lacroix dashes off a sketch which he tosses at a trained team of seamstresses who interpret and realize even his most farfetched inspirations, Alaïa works sometimes late into the night, his mouth full of pins, as he drapes and pulls and turns and twists and dances around the dais like Pygmalion dressing an already transformed and fully alive Galatea.

I remember one night when the Galatea was a ravishing, pouting, smiling teenager, Naomi Campbell, who later would become one of the world's most famous models, but who then was just a sumptuously beautiful shy English adolescent. She kept turning and turning obediently as Azzedine ordered her to do, though when he stuck a pin in her she shouted lustily and tapped the tiny maestro on the head.

That night the chubby, charming, American painter Julian Schnabel was also in attendance, he who'd made his mark by gluing broken crockery to his imposing canvases. He and Azzedine are best friends, although curiously neither can speak the other's language. Julian, who's very rich, invited us all to dinner—and with Azzedine "all" includes his entourage of at least four or five models, his aristocratic German business manager and two or three gofers. Over dinner I asked them how they'd met, and Julian and Azzedine gave me conflicting versions, each happily insulated in his own language. Julian said, "I dropped in on Azzedine's shop with my then wife Jacqueline and asked to see Mr. Alaïa. When he came downstairs I introduced myself and offered to exchange one of my paintings for a fur coat. He was overwhelmed, since obviously one of my paintings is worth twenty fur coats, but he gratefully accepted."

Azzedine's almost simultaneous version: "This man came to my shop and I'm so embarrassed to say it but I'd never heard of him and when he offered me one of his paintings I just shrugged, but Jacqueline was so beautiful I thought I'd love to have her wearing my coat in New York so I agreed."

Each man finished his answer with a big smile, sure he'd just confirmed what the other had said.

Azzedine, who's from Tunisia, hates it if you say he's a typical Arab businessman who lives over the shop, but in fact he bought an immense, four-thousand-square-meter workshop and warehouse that was built in the nineteenth century, and converted it into a boutique, an enormous showroom with a runway for his style shows, a dormitory for the models, workshops for fabricating clothes—and he lives above it, ready to come swooping down at a moment's notice.

Just as dancers like to smoke, models like to eat, and nothing is more delightful than watching Azzedine's cook prepare a succulent leg of lamb covered in mint leaves and coated in honey or some other North African delicacy for these skinny, ravenous beauties.

Over dinner Azzedine loves to speak of the great women he's known or adored from afar. His first idol was the Egyptian singer Um Kulthum, whose concerts would be broadcast on the radio one evening a month throughout the Arab world during the 1950s. The most celebrated and respected Arab performer of this century, she was as worshipped as Maria Callas and as powerful as Margaret Thatcher was at the time of the

Falklands invasion. On the morning of her monthly recital the little Azzedine would be sent to the local café, which possessed the only radio in town, to reserve a chair as near the radio as possible for his grandfather. There his grandfather would install himself with a jasmine flower behind his ear and sigh and weep as Um Kulthum improvised verse after verse, hour after hour, of her lovesick ballads. On that day, once a month, no business was conducted throughout the Arab world, all misdeeds were overlooked, and no war could be fought. Um Kulthum taught Alaïa his first lesson about the power and mystery of female artistry.

When he arrived in Paris in the 1960s he became a private dressmaker to Louise de Vilmorin, a well-known poet and hostess and André Malraux's mistress. Vilmorin had lived for a while in the United States, and her daughter had married and settled there. One day Vilmorin's nine-year-old grandson, whom she'd never seen, was expected, and Vilmorin, ever the seductress, was obsessed about what she should be wearing when the child arrived, where she should be standing, and which profile she should present him with. Azzedine had to advise the coquettish grandmother on every detail. As her confidant, he also got to hear all the gossip about fashionable Paris during the preceding half-century.

His favorite private client was Greta Garbo. Just at

the beginning of the 1970s he was making clothes for Cécile Rothschild, who was living in Coco Chanel's old townhouse on the rue du Faubourg St.-Honoré. One day Cécile said to him, "I have a special customer for you, but if you make a big fuss over her or are indiscreet I'll be very disappointed." Curiously enough, Azzedine had been watching *Queen Christina* on television only the night before, and when he entered Madame Rothschild's salon, there was the same immortal face greeting him.

"At that time," Azzedine recalled, "around 1970, human taste was at a historic low, and since I was part of my era I, too, liked orange and black and horrible fabrics and cuts. Miss Garbo, however, was outside or above history. She wanted me to make her a military greatcoat. She described what she wanted in detail and even gave me the fabric, which was very heavy. At the time I was living in a little room but I made my German business manager walk back and forth in Garbo's coat as we worked through the night, night after night, trying to imagine how the coat would move and drape and how she could bear the weight. But after many fittings and hundreds of suggestions from Miss Garbo, at last the design worked like a charm—and I felt Garbo had *purified* my taste of all the follies of that terrible period."

One of Azzedine's idols was the actress Arletty, star of all those black-and-white prewar films with Michel

Simon. She was the quintessential *parisienne*, with her plucked eyebrows, racy laugh and penetrating, nasal voice always ready to deliver a wisecrack. Jean-Pierre Grédy, the playwright, recently told me that whereas Arletty had the body of a goddess painted by the School of Fontainebleau, her voice was that of a gutter rat. Gérard Depardieu, he pointed out, has exactly the opposite combination of characteristics: his body is that of a peasant, whereas his voice is almost feminine.

By the time Alaïa knew Arletty she was already old and blind, but he revered her. And he'd been directly inspired by the dress she wears in *Hôtel du Nord*, which unzips from top to bottom on the diagonal.

Alaïa has a masterful eye when he turns it on old clothes. In New York once he was led through the clothing archives of the Fashion Institute of Technology and was unimpressed by everything until he suddenly chanced upon beautifully elegant clothes from the 1930s and 1940s. He exclaimed, "But these clothes must have been designed by a European!" The curator told him that in fact they had been designed by Charles James, the great eccentric and, indeed, America's most revered dress designer.

Alaïa was called in by the fashion museum at the Louvre when it wanted to dress some display dummies in dresses from the 1930s made by Madame Vionnet. The curator didn't know what to make of all these odd bits of white fabric, but Azzedine, who'd studied old fashion photos and who admires Vionnet more than any other couturier of the past, was able to drape them and tuck them and fold them expertly and to create an unusually striking display.

His favorite fashion icon, though, he's never met: the Queen Mother. He's awestruck by her fashion sense, especially her penchant for Nile green.

Once Julian Barnes, the English author of *Flaubert's Parrot*, and his wife, Pat Kavanagh, the powerful literary agent, came to visit me in Paris. When I suggested we all go to an Alaïa fashion show, Julian snorted, "Edmund, you've been in Paris too long. Fashion show, indeed!" But Pat and I persuaded him, and he was not only enthralled by the long-legged beauties on the runway but delighted when I introduced him to Alaïa faithful Tina Turner. She exclaimed, "I haven't read *Flaubert's Parrot* yet, but I have it on my bedside table, Mr. Barnes."

CHAPTER IV

The concierge is a disappearing institution, though the memory of this domestic Cerberus and spy remains potent for most Parisians. If someone becomes really detailed, spiteful and petty in his gossip, he's likely to be upbraided with the rhetorical question "What are you, a concierge?" For the French protect their privacy with a sacred fury and prefer the permissiveness of sophisticated silence to the pleasure of spicy gossip (or "crusty," as they say—*croustillant*).

We have a concierge, Madame Denise, who is sweet, funny and, above all, discreet. She lives in her little *loge* at the rear of the courtyard. Her windows are bedecked with impeccably white lace curtains in which swans and swains are picked out in eyelets.

Everyone in the neighborhood likes her. The Indian restaurant a block away gives her curries too strong for her stomach—but not for Fred's. The nearby funeral parlor gives her slightly faded flower arrangements; on some days our narrow, rainy courtyard is carpeted with anthuriums or gladioli or mountains of chrysanthemums denuded of their satin sashes spelling out the name of the deceased. At Christmastime she receives a prematurely browning and shedding pine tree, which she decorates with a string of lights she runs on a cord out from under her door into the part of the courtyard sheltered from the rain.

Madame Denise takes in packages for us but also shipments for the bookstore on the street level, cleverly named Mona Lisait ("Mona was reading," not a bad name for a store selling art books); the boys who work there in return trundle out the garbage can for her every night. But Madame Denise's greatest admirer is the coiffeuse in the shop next to Mona Lisait, a stunning young *beur* (a French-born Arab) who tries out all the latest hairstyles on Madame Denise. One day our concierge will look like a Roman matron, the next like a Neapolitan tart, then a week later she'll become a Tonkinese princess or a cabaret singer of the 1940s, startlingly resembling the imposing, throaty, lesbian chanteuse Suzy Solidor. Of course constant variety is the very source of the *parisienne*'s power to bewitch us, but it's somewhat disconcerting to see your motherly (and normally brunette) concierge coiffed with a bright red punk's coxcomb at eight in the morning (or—to be more honest—at ten).

Madame Denise lives with her son, who looks so solid, so ageless that at first I mistook him for her husband. In fact he looks a bit like the cowardly criminal in a Jean Gabin gangster film, with his pencil-thin mustache, sleeveless yoke-necked T-shirt and surprisingly silent way of walking (or rolling by), as if on casters. To be sure, he's not at all a gangster; on the contrary, he has a medal for twenty-five years of faithful service sweeping up at the town hall, the gleaming white Hôtel de Ville just two blocks away, and his mother showed it to me proudly. We've never seen him with another human being except his mother. "I've tried to persuade him to marry," she says with the cooing regret and feigned annoyance of the Triumphant Mom, "but he's a quiet boy, a real loner, and he's comfortable here."

One of his *relations*, or "contacts," at the Hôtel de Ville is a strange little burn victim with a molting wig and a crablike gait, an old monsieur who works as a bookkeeper for the mayor; he comes once a year to the *loge* to sort out Madame Denise's taxes, and

she in turn prepares for him skate and capers in black butter.

Loge is the word not only for a concierge's apartment but also for an actor's dressing room, and Madame Denise, in her modest, smiling way, has a flair for the theatrical. An excitable French photographer, sent over by British *Vogue*, wanted to set up a shot in which Madame Denise would open her door slightly and with a smile hand me my morning mail while Fred looked on approvingly. We had to repeat this little scene twenty times but each time Madame Denise was just as natural, unaffected, gay—a born star. One day she showed me a glossy German photographic study of the concierges of Paris in which she figures prominently as the genuine French article (most of the few remaining concierges are Portuguese, which means their entryways smell of salted cod, their national dish, instead of *raie au beurre noir*).

Even better, Madame Denise is from the Nord-Pas-de-Calais region, considered the best breeding ground for conscientious, hardworking concierges. She was born in Lille and brought up there, in a boisterous, sentimental, accordion-playing café, and she "descended on" Paris twenty-eight years ago with her husband, who promptly died. Luckily she found her position as a concierge and has held on to it tenaciously ever since. She has never traveled and doesn't seem to approve of

it; she shakes her head tragically whenever we take off for Italy or Nice or London or the States. "Never a moment of repose," she laments. Of course she does her own traveling, through stamp-collecting, and she has my permission to cut out with a big pair of scissors the canceled stamps on my mail from Greece, Austria, Thailand and other exotic places (she loves the *Porgy and Bess* commemorative stamps from the States).

In the afternoon she begins to socialize. She'll stand at the bar of Les Piétons just next door with the whores, all of whom she knows by name. If she's not at Piétons, she's at the other corner bar, the Royal St.-Martin. Sometimes, when we catch her coming back from the bar, she tells us of the famous movie star who used to live in our apartment, and of her many loves. We exchange stories about some of the gallant adventures of our handsome landlord and new "crusty" details about his cheapness; like all Frenchmen he fancies himself a *bricoleur*, a weekend Mr. Fix-it, and would rather attempt five times in a row to repair our leaking hotwater heater than call in a proper plumber.

She knows we're gay and says nothing, but does not resort to the polite fiction used by the restaurateur on the corner of referring to Hubert as my "son" (*votre fiston*), a particularly difficult lie to sustain given my American accent. She also knows Hubert is ill, and when he's in a bad way she'll offer to shop or cook for us;

she asked only once what was wrong with him, and I, in my best French way, became evasive, giving her her cue to retreat into her usual discretion.

She has seen everything in her work and has a name for most of her observations. One day she was washing up some human *merde* left in the entryway, by one of the local bums no doubt. Bright-eyed and uncomprehending, I said, "What's that you're cleaning up, Madame Denise?"

"Une sentinelle, Monsieur" (a sentry).

"What's a *sentinelle*, Madame Denise? I don't know that word."

She turned on me a weary, faintly superior and terminally sophisticated face: "Just think about it another little moment, Monsieur White."

CHAPTER V

One day I received an unexpected phone call. The voice on the other end of the line, though I'd heard it on only one other occasion, and that twelve years before, was unique, unmistakable. "Father Riches!"

I'm not the least bit Catholic, but so powerful is this priest's appeal that one wants to kiss his ring, although that would hardly please him. He's far too fastidious and up-to-date.

When I met Pierre Riches, the place had been New York, the year 1982, and I had just published a gay autobiographical novel, *A Boy's Own Story*, which was enjoying a small success. Father Riches, who was attached to the Vatican and spoke fluent, cultivated English with an indefinable accent, appeared to have been given a special mission (could it be?) to the gay literary community. Or was he a self-appointed lavender curate?

At least he seemed to know the other six gay writers in my literary chat group, the Violet Quill, and to have read our books with the lurid covers which had been shipped hot off the press, perhaps on dry ice, by diplomatic pouch into the very heart of Vatican City. In addition, he spoke easily of Allen Ginsberg and William Burroughs. He was humble and announced that he owned nothing but the clothes on his back and would appreciate dedicated copies of all my future books, but at the same time he came dangerously close to the venial sin of (dare I say it?) name-dropping in his references to "John" (Ashbery) and "Harold" (Brodkey), not to forget "Susan" (Sontag).

I lost track of him and didn't know where to send him my books, although once, about five years ago, someone told me Father Riches had been punished for his overly zealous pastoral work among the gay literati (gliterati?) and had been assigned the poorest parish church in the ugliest suburb of Rome. Still I thought of him occasionally. Just three days before he called me, I mentioned his name to Gary Indiana, the East Village chronicler of punks, junkies and sick queens (in his latest novel two guys take acid and have sex in the ruined

ovens of Auschwitz), and he told me that he, too, had received a visit from the sophisticated priest years ago in his pad on Avenue C.

Although our number in Paris is unlisted, there Pierre Riches was, twelve years later, purring away on the line. I invited him by for tea, delighted to be able to show him off to Hubert.

He arrived, kindly and elegant as ever, his manners superb, his looks unchanged, although now, as he explained, he was past seventy and had retired to a tiny parsonage on Lake Garda, where he still said the odd Mass in the local village chapel. We showed him proudly around our apartment. When he saw the Robert Mapplethorpe portraits of me—rare, since I'm neither naked, nor black nor in toy harness—he said smoothly that Mapplethorpe had once taken a picture of him in his soutane. He admired our gold-and-white Napoleon coffee service, which he identified right away, as well as the Gothic spires of St.-Merri across the street.

Over tea he explained to Hubert that he'd been born a Jew in Egypt. When he was a boy in Alexandria, Cavafy had stroked his hair, and he had also been introduced to E. M. Forster and other local celebrities. He had been brought up in Paris, however, by his Italian father and French mother, before going off to Oxford, where he'd converted to Catholicism. I thought of the society priest who converted the famous *grande cocotte*

Liane de Pougy late in her life by telling her at a dinner party, "Christ shall be your last lover."

For some reason we mentioned William Burroughs; the globe-trotting Father Riches said he'd just come back from Lawrence, Kansas, where he'd observed with pleasure Burroughs feeding his cats, painting his abstract canvases, receiving young admirers and devoting hours to target practice. Father Riches spoke with equal familiarity of David Leavitt (now living in Florence), of Alan Hollinghurst (who had recently brought out his brilliant new gay pedagogical novel, *The Folding Star*, based on Charlotte Brontë's *Villette*), and other members of the gay jet set. It wasn't always clear whether he knew all these writers personally or was merely abreast of their activities.

A few weeks later Hubert (who'd really taken a shine to the worldly man of God) and I were in Bellagio on Lake Como. Pierre Riches came calling on us and led us to the villa where he was staying, an old silk factory now converted into a house by a pious woman of wealth, the president of an international Catholic charity. The lady's handsome sons were lounging naked by the pool and waved at us merrily as we strolled along to the villa. We sat outside, sipping apricot-flavored iced tea and looking at the snow-covered Alps on the other side of the dark blue lake. We could smell cooking meat—supplies his hostess was preparing for the priest to take back to his parsonage. He explained that he'd received a special papal dispensation that allowed him to say Mass in people's houses and just that morning the whole family had celebrated a very intimate and exclusive service at home. I told him he reminded me of an old American friend, Dicky McIntosh, one of whose ancestors had saved the life of a king of England in battle. In return the king had granted him one wish—which in his case was a regal dispensation for him and his descendants never to have to unbonnet before royalty. When Dicky turned twenty-one he traveled all the way from Baltimore to Windsor Castle just to exercise his familial prerogative. He bought a gray hat at Lock's for the occasion.

The story wasn't really very à propos, but Father Riches liked the farfetched comparison and repeated it in Italian to his benefactress.

Allen Ginsberg's latest twenty-year-old came through Paris on his way to Italy not long ago. He phoned and promised to contact me on his way back through town. When he came by a month later he said he'd stayed with Father Riches in his charming parsonage on Lake Garda. The young man shook his head and said, "It was terrible!"

"Really? Did he try to seduce you?" I asked, concerned.

"No. He tried to convert me."

CHAPTER VI

I first met Billy Boy at the Ritz. A young man who has done covers for several of my books in America phoned, saying he'd like to meet me but alas the only time he had free was lunchtime that very same day. I said I was having lunch with two rather stuffy Hollywood producers at the Ritz but he could join us if he liked. He did like, and brought along a glamorous creature sporting purple fingernails and bleached hair piled a foot high. The conservative producers in their gray suits and rep ties looked displeased. I hurried my ill-assorted party off to Davé's, a nearby chic Chinese restaurant frequented by *Vogue* editors and models and run by a self-dramatizing Chinese proprietor who loves to show off photos of his celebrity customers and of himself when he was thinner and given to wearing drag of the slit-silk-skirt variety. Whenever we go there Davé kisses us on the lips, and one night Pierre Le-Tan, the Vietnamese illustrator, and his English wife, Plum, and I speculated on how to avoid this moist collision. Plum and I had no ideas and got roundly bussed, but lucky Pierre went down on one knee and kissed Davé's hand, which delighted our host and spared Pierre another strange encounter of the third kind.

Today Davé was thrilled that Billy Boy, the famous American maker of one-of-a-kind jewels, had graced his restaurant, and he kept furnishing Billy with tall glasses of chilled vodka. Finally the ice was broken at our table when the two producers and Billy Boy all discovered they shared a passion for Barbie Doll.

Billy had started collecting Barbies when he was just a whippersnapper growing up in Staten Island. By now he has some 16,000 and is looking for a château where he can open a private museum to house not only his collections of dolls but also his haute couture dresses from the past. He owns Schiaparelli hats of upside-down shoes and quaintly presented pork chops, as well as the very gown Wallis Simpson wore when she first danced with the future Edward VIII, and the very string of fake bananas Josephine Baker strung about herself when she first conquered Paris.

The day I met Billy, a show he had organized happened to be running. He had commissioned eighty top dress designers to create outfits for Barbie: they were all on display inside a train three cars long at the zoo in the Bois de Boulogne. The two Hollywood producers rushed through their dim sum, and we all piled into their waiting limo and hurried off to Billy's Barbie show. We were the only visitors who weren't three-foot-tall girls.

After that I wrote a story on Billy Boy for *Architectural Digest*. He's what journalists call "good copy." I just took down everything he said and the editors gobbled it up. Billy showed me some of his more important historic dresses. He showed me his Warhol portrait of Barbie. He introduced me to his long-suffering companion, Lala, dressed for the occasion in plus fours and Christian Lacroix sunglasses that gave him an insect head. He showed me around his apartment, which used to belong to the painter Édouard Vuillard. He was already beginning to tire of Barbie, he said, and had invented his own doll, Mdvani, a trendy *parisienne* with lesbian and multiracial friends. As Billy said darkly, peering over the top of his glasses, "Mdvani will not have *unlined* skirts like certain dolls we could name. . . ." To this day, whenever Hubert and I want to reproach each other, we'll start off with the phrase, "*I* always hang up my clothes, *pas comme certaines poupées*. . . ."

Soon after I met Hubert, I gave an all-boy dinner party, which for him was a novelty since he had been quietly married until then. Of the various guests the one who most impressed Hubert was the flamboyant Billy, who arrived in an outfit more appropriate to the high wire than to the *bas-fonds* of big-city nightlife.

Billy dropped out of sight for a moment, but then last autumn I received a frantic call from him: "Darling, I have terrible news. I was nearly *raped* in front of my apartment late one night, a young man *spurted* all over my skirt, I was so traumatized that I sold Billy Boy Enterprises to a multinational, closed the Paris apartment, and Lala and I have moved to Trouville, where we take long walks by the sea and wear only clothes from the 1920s."

CHAPTER VII

I first heard of Pierre Guyotat years ago, while I was still living in New York. Richard Howard, the celebrated poet and translator from the French, told me, "The avant-garde is alive and well in France. No, I'm serious, they still believe in it, and the latest genius, *le vrai génie du moment*, is named Pierre Guyotat, and he's written a magnificent, obsessive, unreadable, *impossible* book called *Eden, Eden, Eden*."

Soon after I moved to France, my friend and translator Gilles Barbedette invited me to dinner with Guyotat, a bald man with an imposing dome and a small dark rosebud of a mouth and a permanent shadow of a beard. He seldom lifted his eyes from the table, and he ate everything in sight, with his white, small-boned hands moving constantly toward his mouth. He ate all his food, then began to pick off my plate and then Gilles's. He never stopped eating, and Gilles was embarrassed and rushed out to find odds and ends in the fridge that he could submit as offerings to Baal, because with his small, intense features inscribed in the lower quarter of his immense pale sphere of a head, with his solid, stubby limbs and barrel chest and his hieratic, mysterious manner, Guyotat resembled a pagan idol, though he ate his food with the tidy *gourmandise* of a grizzly bear.

He spoke constantly of his work and of his life and career. At that time he was finishing a canonical work entitled quite simply *Le Livre* (The Book); it occurred to me that if the Bible is known as the Good Book, his could be known as the Bad Book, since there was possibly something satanic about him. The author of the Bad Book assumed one was already a devotee, so I thought it would be rude to ask him any direct questions, but I gathered from his monologue that his new work, the product of many years' labor, was written not in ordinary French (which he referred to dismissively as *la langue normative*) but in a strange subvocal language of his own devising, one that omitted vowels among other unnecessary luxuries.

At that time I was writing a column for American

Vogue about the cultural life of Paris and mentioned in print that Guyotat was about to publish a landmark in the history of the avant-garde, *Le Livre*. I also suggested to an arty little magazine on the West Coast that it commission a translation of one chapter from this work, and the review was delighted to do so. At Christmas I received a card from Guyotat himself with the message: "This year you have done more for Guyotat than anyone else." I was very gratified.

Years went by and I heard of Guyotat only indirectly. The library in Paris where I was doing research for my biography of Jean Genet also housed Guyotat's archives, and there I met a beautiful but haggard young woman who was writing her thesis on Guyotat and therefore had to make constant burnt offerings to her deity. She told me lots of stories about her evenings and even weekends entertaining the great man. Often she had run errands for him. I asked her if Guyotat was homosexual, but she said his sexuality did not involve other living creatures.

Stephen Barber, the English biographer of Antonin Artaud, came under Guyotat's spell, since he regarded Guyotat as the direct heir to the even more lunatic aspects of Artaud's genius. He invited Guyotat to a mansion where he was house-sitting in Greenwich, but he was dismayed to learn when Guyotat arrived that he intended to stay two months; after a week Stephen cracked and announced that unfortunately his hospitality would be curtailed by the imminent visit of a bedridden grandmother.

Then a couple of years ago Albert Dichy, director of the Jean Genet archives, programmed a series of discussions and readings at the Odéon theater in Paris around the run of a prestigious revival of Genet's play *The Balcony*. Albert considers Guyotat a direct spiritual heir to the more violent and pornographic side of Genet's genius, and he asked him to give a reading.

Guyotat consented. The reading was scheduled for a twenty-minute slot just after a panel discussion and just before the stagehands had to set up for that night's performance of *The Balcony*. When Albert told Guyotat he'd have only twenty minutes to read, the writer replied loftily, "But time is inscribed *within* the interior of the work and has no independent exterior existence." Albert swallowed hard.

Bald head gleaming under the spotlights, Guyotat began to intone in his own tongue, scrupulously avoiding any concession to the normative language. His hands moved rhythmically and beautifully as though he were the sibyl inhaling the sacred fumes and swaying above the tripod in a trance. In his language every other word sounded like "testicles" for some reason. The impious in the audience fled in droves, leaving behind only hardcore devotees.

Backstage another drama was brewing. As the twenty-minute limit was approaching, the stage manager told Albert that he couldn't let the reading go over, not even a minute or two. After all, he had a whole team of union stagehands to supervise and their work time was quantified down to the last second. Still Guyotat intoned on dreamily, his hands writhing like the serpents around the caduceus. The stage manager announced he was going out now to remove the poet forcibly from his pulpit. Albert protested that if the stage manager did any such thing the rest of the Genet festival would be canceled. Just as the two men were about to come to blows, the time inscribed within the interior of the work mysteriously ripened and the high priest swept off, to the ecstatic applause of the woman writing her thesis, Stephen Barber, Albert's wife, Hubert and me. The rest of the shallow audience had evaporated.

Hubert and I live only a block from the Centre Georges Pompidou, where cultural events are frequently programmed into the large hall in the basement. When my Genet book came out, there were five successive evenings devoted to such subjects as Genet and the cinema, Genet and politics, Genet and homosexuality, and so on. Before this Genet festival, however, Guyotat announced he'd be staging his own five-day festival. Each night he would improvise prose live before an audience. For this event he graciously conceded to

speak in the normative language. Catherine, the woman writing her thesis on Guyotat, was there every night, of course, taping every word, and Albert, who was handling the Guyotat archives, was also in constant attendance. The great man had not announced how long he'd be speaking on any given evening; on some nights his inspiration gave out after thirty minutes, but the lucky audience on another evening had a full three-hour improvisation.

He was dressed in black trousers and a black shirt and jacket. His eyelids were half closed. His hands were weaving the air before him. As he spoke, he created a vision of a foul dog writhing in the filth of primeval slime, belly huge and erotically bulging, the trademark testicles much dwelled on. There was a conflict of some sort with higher creatures in the eternal night. Prostitution, rifle butts and testicles were recurring themes. It had been a long day, and soon I was dozing, blending Guyotat's words into a dream vision of Milton's Lucifer, bedecked for the occasion with a pair of bright red Christmas balls. Hubert, I'm ashamed to say, was wide awake for the entire two hours and seventeen minutes.

CHAPTER VIII

Everyone in Paris seems to be the son or grand-daughter or nephew of someone famous. The famous people themselves belong to the city's glorious past; their relatives, like Parisians in general, are living off their patrimony. Of course, Americans are always swooning over aristocratic titles, but what else is a count or a duke except the descendant of some medieval (or Napoleonic) bully who managed to confiscate other people's property or impress defenseless peasants into his service? At least the children of artists have a more admirable claim to fame. Their famous forebears were brilliant, and their children stand a chance of having acquired some talent along the way—or at least a good anecdote or two.

Ivan Nabokov is my editor in Paris. His father, the composer Nicholas Nabokov, who wrote the lackluster score for Balanchine's *Don Quixote*, was a distant cousin of Vladimir Nabokov's. Ivan himself shared a room at Harvard with Vladimir's son, Dmitri, who lives in Montreux, Switzerland, but who passes through Paris rather frequently. Whereas Dmitri is a playboy famous for his fast cars and beautiful women, Ivan is a quiet, bookish man whose one extravagance is his clothes. He's often called the most elegant man in Paris. He's spent so much of his life reading that he has ruined his eyes and recognizes no one in the street. Perhaps that's why he's so hail-fellow-well-met—he's afraid of appearing to snub an acquaintance, and God knows the French are quick to feel slighted. Ivan's father was married a number of times. Ivan is the son of Nicholas's first wife, a Russian from a very noble family who eventually went to live in the United States and became an announcer for Radio Free Europe. Nicholas's last wife, Dominique, is much younger than her stepson Ivan. She's French but lives most of the time in New York, where she works as a photographer for *Vogue*, which until recently was under the direction of Nicholas's old Russian friend Alexander Lieberman.

Ivan mumbles terribly. English and Americans

assume he can't speak their language properly, while the French assume he's not entirely at home in their language. In fact, he's a normally quadrilingual Russian, equally at ease in Russian, German, French and English, although English is the only *written* language he's fully mastered, since it's the one he did his studies in. No, in speaking his only problem is that he mumbles.

His wife, Claude, also mumbles. Her last name is Joxe and her brother was minister of the interior under Mitterrand and her father a minister under de Gaulle. Her family has lived for centuries in the same house in the place Dauphine on the Île de la Cité, and she and her relatives continue to live in that house, just across the river from us. Claude is a professional researcher, especially of pictures; in French such a person is called an *iconographe*, a suitably Russian title for the wife of a Nabokov—or Nabokoff, as the French spell it. Ivan is now changing his citizenship from American to French and has requested that the spelling of his name be changed accordingly; he received, however, an official letter from the French immigration department telling him that he must preserve the name in its English spelling, which the officials incorrectly assumed was the Russian spelling.

Another Claude we know is Claude Picasso, the brother of the more formidable Paloma. I once introduced a smiling, gushing young woman from California to Paloma. After they talked together for half an hour the Californian couldn't resist saying, "You're so much sweeter than you look in your pictures!" Paloma surprised me by replying, "I'm so short that I discovered if I start out nice everyone walks all over me, whereas if I start out mean people are intimidated and I can gradually warm up and make a better impression."

Claude is also short, but he's nice all the time to everyone. Way back in the early 1970s, before he'd received his inheritance and while he was still working as a photographer to support himself, I was an editor of a magazine and hired him to photograph famous painters and the things they collected (Andy Warhol and his Aunt Jemima cookie jars, for instance, or Walter Darby Bannard and his scrimshaw collection). When I met Claude again in Paris in the 1980s he remembered our professional encounter, although, bizarrely enough, I didn't. I'm often accused of being a great namedropper, but imagine forgetting a name like Picasso!

Claude has an American wife named Sydney, who used to be married to a French aristocrat. Sydney is a slender redhead who wore flashy haute couture dresses in the 1980s, but in the 1990s she finds such frivolities offensive and clothes herself in loose dark suits and exquisite jewelry made for her by artists.

Or by Marcial Berro. Marcial is a microscopically small and ageless Argentinian who used to go everywhere with Paloma, her tiny Argentinian husband and another minuscule Argentinian friend. They were collectively known as "Paloma and the Palomettes."

I first met Marcial in the early 1970s, in what was once a maid's room in the former Ansonia Hotel in New York. We were having Sunday brunch at someone's apartment and Marcial had just arrived from Buenos Aires. He couldn't speak very much English, but he had a stack of old 78 tango records. He grabbed the equally small girl who'd come with me and trotted her all over the apartment, a low-ceilinged room right under the eaves that looked over the housetops toward Central Park. During each life only a few romantic moments are granted; for me one occurred that morning, when the maid's room smelled of coffee and Gitanes, a parrot was hopping into and out of his cage, and Marcial was dipping and pivoting so stylishly to those lovesick tangos. He told me there was nothing more moving than watching cowboys in the pampas dancing the tango, hot tears streaming down their lined, tanned faces.

In Paris, Marcial made a name for himself as a jeweler—in fact the best jeweler of all in this fastidious, narcissistic and fad-enslaved city. Only a trained eye could distinguish his rings and earbobs, which are simplicity itself, from those of countless imitators. Now he's designing household objects as well, including a silver champagne cooler that breaks out in big silver boils.

Claude and Sydney have always kept busy cataloging his immense Picasso collection (the pottery alone!) and he makes sure sleazy manufacturers don't appropriate without a license the *Demoiselles d'Avignon* for bedspreads or the *Guernica* for underwear. Time-consuming as all these projects were, people were still impertinent enough to wonder when Picasso would begin to . . . *paint*.

So intimidating is such a prospect that Claude has had to buy an entire Greek island, heavily guarded, where he paints in secret. What he does let the public see are his rug designs, which have all the verve and panache his name might suggest.

I once introduced Claude Picasso to Rachel Stella, Frank Stella's daughter. As we went down the stairs to dinner, I whispered stagily to Claude, "Her father, you know, is a very famous painter."

Rachel is also the daughter of the art critic Barbara Rose, who has a mania for buying one small, unsuitable apartment in Paris and selling it to buy another. I met Rachel while she was squatting her mother's dim concierge's *loge* on the Île St.-Louis. Soon she was living in a 1960s basement off the place Maubert, next to a weird cafeteria (which the French, showing off their mastery of English, call a "self "). Since I write by hand and my hand is illegible, I have to hire a typist, to whom I dictate my manuscripts. For weeks one winter I dictated my novel *The Beautiful Room Is Empty* to Rachel in that 1960s basement while her ancient chow dog paced arthritically over the cold stone floor and stuck out her blue tongue at us. Whenever Rachel frowned I panicked and reworked the offensive sentence.

That experience drew us closer. One night I invited her to dinner with Pierre Aubry, the documentary filmmaker, and his girlfriend, a Japanese woman who promised to translate my fiction into Japanese. But Pierre and Rachel had fallen in love at first sight, within a week were living with each other, months later were married, and soon were blessed with Rebekah Edmonde, my adorable goddaughter. The Japanese woman sent me a note a week after that fateful encounter and said that for health reasons she would be unable to translate my works. I must say I understood her reluctance. To be sure, it had never occurred to me that Rachel and Pierre would fall in love with each other.

Rachel has a big, by-appointment-only gallery in Auteuil, where she sells works on paper by contemporary artists. Her husband makes movies about "marginal" writers, and he invites all his subjects to his wife's parties. These writers are so recherché—Juan Goytisolo from Spain, Kenji Nakagami from Japan, Ismail Kadare from Albania, Edmund White from the United States—that we're all anything but household names, and poor Rachel has to work extra hard selling modern art to people who already have walls full of Fragonards and Hubert Roberts. Her worries would be over, of course, if her father were to give her just one of those hideous sculptures he makes that look like explosions in a Frigidaire factory, but Rachel says he needs every penny to feed his polo ponies.

Unfortunately for Rachel, the French—unlike the Germans or the Italians or especially the Greeks—are tightfisted collectors who have horrible taste and complete confidence in it. After all, France is the country that has honored the four worst living artists—Arman, Botero, César, and Bernard Buffet.

To our dinners for the wives and offspring of the celebrated (and over the years we've met tons of them: the granddaughter of Gallimard editor and writer Jean Paulhan; Georges Perec's first wife, now a librarian; the widow of Gaëtan Picon, the critic; Lady Antonia Fraser's daughter Natasha), we liked to invite Hemingway's grandson Ed. He'd been a student at the Rhode Island School of Design while I was teaching at Brown, and then he moved to Paris. Since he makes strange, unhealthy-looking dolls, I thought he might be able to work for Billy Boy, but they quickly came to loathe each other. Billy Boy does a very good Ed Hemingway imitation.

Ed is tall, smiling, handsome and in his early twenties.

He wears the same clothes every day and rarely bathes, but fortunately he swims a lot. When he was a child in New York his mother would go off to work and his father would dress up in her clothes and push the carriage in the park, hoping to pass himself off to the mothers watching their children as his child's mom rather than dad. Since he was a huntin', shootin', football-playin' he-man, probably few of the new mothers were fooled, but Greenwich Village tolerates all sorts of eccentricities. When Ed's mother, a strict Catholic from Ireland, caught on, she blamed the Village and decided they should all move out to Montana, where surely a closer contact with nature would dispel these big-city vices.

But soon Ed's father was getting itchy and begged his wife to go out on the town with him, both of them dressed in her frocks, which wasn't exactly her idea of a fun Saturday night. He drifted away, was arrested for transvestism in a small southern town, had breast implants and then tore them out, and was terrified that another man might be attracted to him—terrified since his fantasies were anything but homosexual.

Ed emerged out of all that as a nice, normal homosexual, but his mother, in spite of everything, remains a respectable Catholic lady. She came to dinner with her brother from Dublin and seemed slightly ill at ease being entertained by a male couple, Hubert and me,

even though she's obviously making efforts to accept her son's world. Nevertheless she seemed distinctly relieved when a bright, seemingly conventional group of French friends dropped in after dinner—Bernard, a playwright; yet another Claude, a novelist and biographer; Philippe, a film producer; and his wife, Anne, who used to be a model and now directs films. When they left, Mrs. Hemingway asked conversationally, "Who were those lovely people?" I couldn't resist saying, "Bernard used to be lovers with Claude, but Claude is now Anne's lover, though she's married to his best friend, Philippe. They all go everywhere together."

I hope this book is never translated into French, because the French would thoroughly disapprove of this chapter. They dislike name-dropping so much they don't even have a word for it.

CHAPTER IX

In this drawing of our local gay and lesbian bookshop, Les Mots à la Bouche, Hubert is daring to suggest that my books and other "literary" works of queer fiction are usually remaindered, whereas customers throng to the shelves selling pornography. Let me set the record straight. My books did languish a bit when they had discreet covers, but Ivan Nabokov, my editor, who isn't even gay, repackaged them all with sexy black-and-white photos and now they fly off the shelves.

It is true the store is full of gay writers pretending to look through serious new novels and criticism before they sidle back to the skin rags—or to the fateful corner where their own books should be displayed. I've seen

some pretty nasty scenes if the author discovers his own classic novel has vanished to make way for some vulgar current bestseller. Then the patient, polite bookseller, Jean-Pierre Meyer-Genton, invents stories about a mixup at the warehouse, a truck drivers' strike or an imminent reprint.

Hubert and I really don't know anything about the gay scene in the Marais, although it is swirling all around us. The Marais may be a quiet area of old houses, art galleries and bookstores, but it's also a magnet for gay Parisians. Wolf packs of guys in leather or jeans, their hair long and silky on top, shaved military style below all the way up to the temple, stalk down the rue des Lombards. They are there on their way from the Quetzal Bar on the rue des Mauvais Garçons (Bad Boys' Street), which quietly booms behind its new bossed and brushed chrome façade like a party in a submerged submarine, to the Banana Café in Les Halles with its go-go boys and imposing lesbian proprietor. Anything I might say about the bars or their customers would be based on hearsay. Fred takes no more interest in the Kiki Boys than I do, unless they're walking a dog—which already sets them apart as neighbors, not Bad Boys, as nice quiet bachelors out walking Bichonnet or Macho Adoré. These are men with whom one can have a pleasant chat about the hardheaded (*têtu*) basset hound versus the crazy (*fou-fou*) terrier.

CHAPTER X

Our neighborhood, the Châtelet, is character-
less by day, more a corridor between the
shops and restaurants of Les Halles and the
boutiques and bistros of the Marais than a
proper place of its own. At night, however, it resumes
its identity as one of the oldest parts of Paris. Our
street, the rue St.-Martin, for instance, was built by the
Romans as their main north-south route. The next
street over, the rue Quincampoix, is just the width of a
car, and at least in the stretch near our house, the huge
seventeenth-century doors, lacquered teal blue or just
treated with clear varnish to show the natural wood,
lead into narrow courtyards and dark stairways.

Often when I go out at night with Fred we collide with the guys carrying into Mona Lisait the books they display on the sidewalk by day, and I run into a thin woman with white hair who I'd guess is close to seventy except she likes to run in sneakers—she says in order to tire her small, excitable puppy, Trompette. When she's not running she'll stroll along beside us while Trompette runs circles around Fred, who looks both smiling and sad, as though he'd love to play, if only she'd slow down to a proper, stately, basset rhythm.

Trompette's owner tells me she's lived in the Châtelet all her life and before she retired she was an usher (*une ouvreuse*) at the Théâtre Musical de Paris (which everyone calls just "the Châtelet") when it performed fun operettas and musical comedies, before it turned to grand opera (such as the current Wagner cycle) and symphony concerts. She recalls that when Les Halles was still the food market of Paris, even the rue St.-Martin was stacked high with rabbit cages and cartons of vegetables. She points out a walled-up building on the rue des Lombards where, she says, a theater troupe of squatters performed until just recently. "It was really *sympathique*. They even had performances for children on Wednesday afternoons; I'd bring my grandniece. No electricity, of course, so they acted by candlelight. You paid what you could, and even if you gave them nothing at all they didn't grumble. Naturally, an easygoing, utopian group like that has no way of keeping out the bad element, so soon there were drug addicts and even thieves, and the fire department closed them down and had the windows and doors bricked in, though they say a few hoboes still live in there. They must have a tunnel in."

One night we were approached by a homeless woman. Trompette's mistress said, "I never give them money, but I will go into the grocery store and buy them a sandwich. Once this woman was very belligerent with me when I did that, since what she wanted was wine. She and her husband, that tall guy with the long hair and dirty beard, have been here for years—they're the ones with the magnificent Russian wolfhound. They all lived around the corner with my friend Hervé in his one-room apartment. He took them in out of friendship. But when he died last year his wife threw them out. The husband with the beard has an apartment in the suburbs. I once saw him all dressed up at a restaurant in the Seventeenth Arrondissement."

The Châtelet is the very heart of Paris, a bit like what Piccadilly Circus is to London or Times Square is to New York. At one corner of the neighborhood is the Centre Georges Pompidou, that massive oil refinery posing as a museum of modern art. When Hubert and I met Richard Rogers, the architect, in London, I said, "Oh, we live just next door to your museum," and he said, "And it's *not* rusting." I never liked the museum before I met him, but he was so charming and his American wife, Ruthie, gave us such a great meal at her restaurant, the River Café, right next to the Thames, and Hubert was so starry-eyed about meeting such a great architect (did I mention that Hubert is an architect?)—that now of course I love the museum. When I used to object to it, Parisian friends would say, "Edmund, you're like those people who objected to the Eiffel Tower." My main quibble in the old days before we met Richard Rogers was that it was rusting, but now of course I've learned not to say that. It appears the whole museum is being shut down for major repairs, which are needed in part because of the volume of visitors—*much* heavier than anyone ever anticipated.

It attracts busloads of tourists from Germany, Holland, England, and now even from Hungary, the Czech Republic and Poland. If the Pompidou draws more tourists than any other French monument, including the Eiffel Tower, that's because it's free—at least the escalator ride to the top is free. Also free are the ground-floor exhibits and stores and the library— where you can roam through the open stacks (quite a rarity in France). Of course you have to pay to get into the upstairs galleries, but few people brave them. For the cost of a coffee you can sit at a table and look in one direction up to the heights of Montmartre, where the

pale dome of Sacré-Coeur glows against the sky like the Taj Mahal; or west to the upended hairpin of the Eiffel Tower; or south to the twin square towers of Notre-Dame and, beyond, to the hideous Montparnasse Tower. That monstrosity was built in the late 1960s by an American named Tuttle, the father of a brilliant young journalist I knew, Alexandra Tuttle, whose plane was shot down recently over the former Soviet Union as it was leaving one embattled republic for another. Alexandra had been a Rhodes scholar, she knew Latin and Greek and read everything, old and new, in every language, but she was enthralled by the glamour of being a real tough reporter, not just a namby-pamby cultural commentator. She had a low voice and a journalist's abrupt way of asking very personal questions. She was in her late twenties when she died, though she had acquired the ageless, timeless manner of a sophisticated Lauren Bacall character, if that character is also granted a fine, well-stocked mind.

Hubert and Fred and I love to wander into the Marais with its seventeenth-century townhouses, although Fred, easygoing as he might be, gets a bit vexed if I pull on his leash too hard and too often in the crowded, narrow streets as we thread our way through the traffic. We keep trying to give him a normal, civilized collar, but he's so strong and hardheaded, not to mention distractible, that we invariably revert to a cruel steel choker, which he doesn't seem to mind. As Hubert becomes frailer and frailer and Fred even heftier, we keep worrying that one day Fred will spot an alluring dog in the distance, go ballistic and drag a hundred-twenty-pound Hubert along behind him. No chance he could drag me down, with my additional hundred pounds of ballast.

On the get-tough leash, however, Fred is still a joy to explore the Marais with, especially the Jewish quarter along the rue des Rosiers with its exotic smells. In warm weather we love eating outdoors at Jo Goldenberg, though this restaurant can be equally pleasant in the winter—in fact wonderfully cozy with its steaming bowls of chicken soup and matzoh balls and its goulash and poppy-seed cake, its strolling gypsy violinists and palm readers, its pair of lazy, overfed dogs and its floor-to-ceiling paintings of rabbis in their prayer shawls or of near-Chagall blue horses and flying musicians. You enter through the delicatessen with its sticky trays of baklava, its tub of pickles in brine and its hunks of corned beef and pastrami or platters of duck with groats. The delicatessen and the long, narrow lunch counter next to it are lit in bluest neon and the floors are of white tile, but the dining room, two steps down, is lined in brown velveteen and dimly lit and is the very definition of *Gemütlichkeit*.

This is one of the few restaurants in Paris where French people actually speak to strangers. I once met a charming woman doctor there, an anesthesiologist for children, by asking her an impertinent question: "Why are you speaking Italian with no accent—and none of the usual music?" She laughed and said, "Because I'm French but my father was Italian and this young woman is my cousin from Bologna, who doesn't speak French. It's true, my Italian is as colorless as it is fluent. No one," she added, laughing harder, "could accuse your French of being either fluent or colorless."

One time the very friendliness of Goldenberg's provoked an excruciatingly embarrassing situation. I had met a young divinity student in Berlin, where I'd given a reading in a gay bookstore, the Prinz Eisenherz, and he'd invited me to his apartment. He was all Adam's apple, anarchistic steel-rimmed glasses and long, spungold Memling hair. When we arrived at his place he asked me solemnly, "Do you want to sleep with me?" "Actually, I just want to sleep," I said, since I'd been traveling from one German city to another on a promotional tour and I was exhausted. He smiled, put me to bed for a nap and prepared something to eat out of potatoes, bratwurst, apples and cumin seeds, which certainly provided a break from French cuisine. After eating, I raced off to another appointment, but we corresponded and soon he announced he was coming to stay with me in Paris.

The minute he arrived I realized that he was not a well

lad—that he wasn't just eccentric but totally bonkers. Though he was blond and blue-eyed and the descendant of generations of Lutheran pastors (he himself intended to become a pastor), he'd somehow convinced himself he was Jewish. He fervently believed that his grandparents had disguised their Jewish origins in order to escape Nazi persecution, but when pressed he couldn't give a single piece of evidence for this plausible-enough possibility other than some vague intuition on his part, some murmurings of his blood or body or subconscious.

Indulging him, I suggested we go to Goldenberg's, where he might be able to pick up a vibe or two. As we were speaking to each other in English, the woman eating alone at the next table admitted as to how she, too, spoke English, and so we were off on a pleasant, three-way conversation, all the more lively when the young German said how much he liked the rue des Rosiers with its little shops, such as one selling menorahs and records of Jewish cantors (now a dress shop), or another with its old steam bath (now a Santa Fe boutique, although the blue ceramic bricks over the door still spell out *Bains-Douches*), and its mitteleuropean food stores on the south side of the street and Middle Eastern food stores on the north. The woman appreciated his observations, but warned us that a ghetto invites pogroms and that this very restaurant had been bombed by terrorists at the beginning of the 1980s.

Suddenly my German guest began to weep. He confessed that he was Jewish, or rather that he strongly suspected he was Jewish, that everything around us seemed a dreamlike distortion of racial memories his cowardly grandparents had tried to erase. And the more he raved the angrier the woman became, until she finally exploded and announced that she'd had it with lunatic German gentiles and their morbid fantasies born out of monstrous mutations of guilt. She made no move to leave, but she did position her chair at an angle away from us and ate in red-faced silence.

The next day I left early to go to Tours to do research on Jean Genet's adolescent imprisonment at a nearby reform school, work for a biography I was writing. When I came back to Paris that evening I found all the lights on at home, a recording of the Kol Nidre playing at full blast, but no sight of my German guest. Then I heard a sob and discovered him sitting naked on the floor before a mirror. He was searching for the Jew in his face and body. Since he'd already announced he would be staying with me for a week, I thought quick and said, "You know, there's a very cheap hotel run by a Jewish family on the rue des Écouffes near Goldenberg's where you might want to continue your . . . research." To my surprise he was delighted by this suggestion, and the very next morning I walked him over and made sure he was comfortably settled. Soon he was mooning over the proprietor's grandmother as she ironed the sheets; he was certain he had known her, or someone like her, in another life. I wheedled my friend Christine Davenier into taking him out to lunch—without me—and I planned other activities for him that would give me some respite, but inevitably we ended up every evening at Goldenberg's, where he was always sniffing the air in search of the religious scent or the cultural spoor.

When he finally went back to Berlin I was so relieved to be rid of him that I didn't answer any of his long, tortured letters, though I did read them—with growing dread, in fact, as he became more and more belligerent because of my silence. One day I received a package from him which contained, quite simply, a human *merde*, presumably his own, wrapped in newspaper.

Hubert protects me now from various nut cases, but I'd met the German back in the 1980s, when I was living alone on the Île St.-Louis, just across the street from a church, St.-Louis-en-l'Île, with its white-and-gold interior, its curious perforated steeple through which you can see the sky, and its roof contained between immense stone volutes. My windows looked out on the snail-shaped volutes, and when I had to move, Hubert (whom I'd just met) did a wonderful drawing of them in sepia ink, which he gave me.

The Île St.-Louis is the most perfect ensemble of

seventeenth-century architecture one can imagine. For centuries the monks of Notre-Dame grazed their cows here (it was even called the Île des Vaches), but in the seventeenth century a group of speculators decided to "develop" the island all at once. One of them was a certain Monsieur Marie, after whom the Pont Marie, the most poetic bridge in Paris, is named. Another developer was Monsieur Le Regrattier, who gave his name to one of the north-south streets, where Christine lives now. My street, the rue Poulletier, was named after a third developer.

Although the mansions along the *quais* were always prized, the inner houses and apartments and the island itself were a bit forgotten and were decidedly *populaire*. Yet there were always notable residents. Baudelaire and Gautier lived here and smoked dope here, and Proust's character Swann lived on the island as well. In the Hôtel Lambert, at the eastern end of the island, Voltaire was once a guest of aristocratic patrons, and in the nineteenth century, Chopin played there for the exiled Polish queen, whose residence it was.

The Rothschilds live in the house now. When they gave up their château in the country, they consoled themselves by buying the Hôtel Lambert, which must be the most perfect house in the city, what with its large walled garden and its celebrated Hercules gallery. Sometimes the rest of us on the island felt a bit like peasants living at the foot of the château. I can remember the day former President Reagan and his wife, Nancy, came to lunch. The Rothschilds' chef, whom I knew slightly, confided to me that the entire staff was in a fever of activity, and my butcher told me proudly that he'd provided the partridges. When I went past his shop at five in the afternoon, he rushed out to tell me the partridges had been a success and Mr. Reagan had even taken seconds.

I've often regretted losing that butcher, who not only was handsome and fabulously expensive but made me appear to be an accomplished cook. He'd wrap chunks of rabbit in some sort of translucent stomach lining and dunk the whole in a light mustard sauce. Following his instructions, I'd cook the rabbit in white wine for forty minutes in the oven, then add *crème fraîche* to make the final sauce. This dish was so easy and I ate it so often that I once apologized to Adam Mars-Jones, the English novelist, for not coming up with anything better for him; he teases me about it to this day ("Just mustard rabbit for lunch, I'm afraid").

My butcher, if given a day's warning, could also make an oven-ready *veau Prince Orloff*. He'd slice a raw veal roast, interleave it with slices of Canadian bacon and cheese, then reconstitute everything inside a caul, or perhaps it was intestines. Since he was a leftist he'd refer to the dish democratically as *veau Orloff*. Despite his politics, he had a taste for luxury. Once I was taking the crowded ferryboat between La Rochelle and the Île de Ré, when a huge yacht roared past, my handsome butcher at the helm, his red cheeks even redder.

There was a sweets shop near me where a fat, unsmiling woman, whom everyone said was an adept of black magic, had revived the art of casting chocolate in creepy, elaborate molds from the nineteenth century. One of her specialties was a waning chocolate moon crossed by a chocolate witch on a chocolate broom.

Madame Pompidou lived nearby, as did Claude Mauriac, the son of the famous novelist François Mauriac. His wife was Proust's grandniece, and these historic associations were never far from my thoughts when I interviewed them about their brief friendship with Jean Genet. When Genet met Madame Mauriac, he said in his most courtly manner, "*Mes hommages à Madame Votre Mère.*" Nearby lives one of Genet's first publishers, Marc Barbezat, and his Montenegrin wife, the fascinating actress Olga. All the lamps and tables and even the bookshelves were made by the sculptor Alberto Giacometti or his brother Diego. Olga is deaf and Marc crippled, but their conversation is sparkling, their memories perfect and their curiosity limitless. Olga has a fiery temper (she and Genet admired each other—and fought fiercely), which Marc sets off nicely with his Swiss Calvinist sobriety.

My landlady on the Île St.-Louis, Madame Pflaum,

lived just downstairs from me. She was a tall Austrian lady who'd first come to Paris in the 1930s to study art. My furnished apartment was decorated with several abstract tapestries from her Montmartre days. She once invited me for tea with her best friend, a woman she'd known for fifty years, and they addressed each other with the formal form of "you," *vous*, instead of the more intimate *tu*, which astonished me. Madame Pflaum's husband had been a celebrated epigraphist, a scholar of Latin inscriptions, and the walls of my entry-way were covered with Latin letters and numbers incised in white marble.

He had excavated these stones in a village in North Africa, a former Roman outpost. Madame Pflaum had grown bored sitting around as her husband dug up stones, and finally she'd decided she'd use her consid-erable energies to help the village out of its misery. She'd taken slides of the needy people and their primi-tive surroundings and traveled all over Europe showing the slides and raising funds. She built sewers and a hos-pital and even sold the villagers' handicrafts abroad. All that had been thirty years before, but even when I knew her she still went to "her" village once a year. During the war, Madame Pflaum, who was Gentile, hid her Jewish husband in a hayloft in the south of France and worked as a field hand. She brought him nourishment every day in the strictest secrecy. She couldn't also look after her child, so she confined her to an orphanage. The daughter, whom I know well, could never entirely forgive her mother for abandoning her.

Toward the end of my seven years on the Île St.-Louis, Madame Pflaum began to suffer from the effects of Alzheimer's disease. I'd find her lost in the stairwell trying to locate her door. She stopped speaking English to me and addressed me only in French, then only in German as she sank back to her linguistic roots. One day she came flying out of her apartment and begged me to save her from her private nurse, who was abusing her. All a fantasy in her disordered mind.

At last she died. The Mass said for her in the white-and-gold splendor of the Église St.-Louis-en-l'Île was so dignified and authentic (the choir sang the seraphic conclusion to Fauré's consoling *Requiem*) that I wished I were Catholic or at least French so that I'd have something to look forward to. Even the priest's remarks about Madame Pflaum were so eloquent, understated and *accurate* that I was puzzled—until Madame Pflaum's daughter explained to me that she herself had written the text about her mother.

The calm of the Île St.-Louis is routinely shattered by two establishments. A restaurant, Nos Ancêtres les Gaulois, serves diners all the free wine they can drink, and toward one in the morning the rue St.-Louis-en-l'Île is full of vomiting English, Irish and German tourists, often brawling or caterwauling their national songs. The other establishment is a sherbet and ice cream maker, Berthillon, the best in Paris (its very best flavor is pear-and-candied-chestnut sherbet). It's so successful it *closes* for part of July and all of August—a typically Parisian bit of effrontery comparable to that of those three-star restaurants which close on the weekend. On a warm spring or autumn day, however, Berthillon will attract *hundreds* of idle, sheeplike people willing to wait an hour for an ice cream cone. Such docility used to make my already chilly puritanical blood run glacially cold.

Not long ago, Hubert and Fred and I ran into Madame Pflaum's daughter as we were waiting patiently in line for a Berthillon cone (try the *gianduja* if you like erotically dark chocolate mined with orange peel, or sample the lip-contracting cassis sherbet). She invited us up to see how she'd remodeled my old apartment and her mother's.

Nothing was the same. The wooden cupboards and space heaters and marble inscriptions and Montmartre tapestries and the dingy kitchen painted hospital green and the cramped bathroom with the small tub were all gone, replaced by recessed lighting and fine cabinets and Carrara marble and gold-necked swan faucets right out of the Ritz, as though a homely but *sympathique* frog had been magically changed into a standard-issue prince. Hubert was nice enough to say the new apartment lacked the charm of my old one.

Although there is a plaque to indicate where even Madame de Sévigné's *cousin* once lived on the Île St.-Louis (and not even a scandalous, literary cousin like Bussy-Rabutin, banned for lampooning members of the court in his *Amorous History of the Gauls*), there's no plaque for James Jones, the American novelist who lived here for years. This omission is all the more serious in that Jones, after previously writing gutsy, good novels such as *From Here to Eternity* while living in the States, foundered completely in Paris. Not only was he uprooted from one country to another, but also he had suddenly risen too many social notches and had nothing interesting to say in his novels about his new rich friends. Some American novelists flourish in Paris (James Baldwin wrote most of his books in Paris or Istanbul), whereas others go to seed. Camus once remarked that American writers are the only ones in the world who are not intellectuals; his observation applies to Jones, who went dry when separated from the ordinary Americans he had written about. It does not apply to the far more intellectual Baldwin, as much an essayist as a novelist, who identified with Henry James and believed that only in Europe did one discover America.

Coming back toward our apartment we usually cross from the Île St.-Louis to the Île de la Cité, wander past

Notre-Dame and then through the flower market (on Sundays a songbird market), before taking the Pont du Change directly to the place du Châtelet. I always stop to talk to a robust, red-faced flower seller from Ireland because she teases me about my accent, though hers sounds just as peculiar. Although Fred was born in the States, he was raised in Paris and now he's too French to understand the pleasures of pointless flirting with strangers, so he usually starts tugging on his leash to spare me from further embarrassing myself.

If we make this circuit on a winter night all the familiar sights are eerily transformed. There's no stranger phenomenon than to walk down the canyonlike rue St.-Louis-en-l'Île and to see the lights of a *bateau mouche* passing between the two islands. There are buildings in the foreground and buildings in the background, the river and the boats themselves are blocked from view, but welling up out of the concealed orchestra pit, as it were, is the splendor of these daylight-bright moving projectors, as flowing and transforming as music. It's like living through a speeded-up total eclipse. The lights are so brilliant that they trace each twig on each bare winter tree against the gliding backdrop of the pale gray house fronts.

On a foggy night the lights in front of Notre-Dame project axonometric drawings of the towers high up into the cloudy sky. The two islands are five degrees

84

colder and wetter than the mainland. In the old days there were *insulaires*, apparently, who seldom went over "to Paris," as they put it, and when I first arrived, there was still an old laundress who used flatirons, one after another, that she warmed on an electrified lazy Susan; she insisted she couldn't control the temperature of a modern self-heating iron half as well. And there were old people who lived in sixth-floor maids' rooms who had to bathe at the public baths on the rue des Deux-Ponts. Now, of course, the island is full of rich people, including many rich Americans, who feel somehow safer and snugger on the Île St.-Louis, as though it were a less threatening and more comprehensible Manhattan. Unfortunately, few of these people live here year-round, and their apartments, which they consider investments, sit dark and empty, especially during the winter months. The shopkeepers complain of the dwindling trade, and one by one they're closing down. The lady who sold horse meat ("Very healthy and clean and digestible," Hubert assures me, "ideal for people who are ill") under the emblem of a beautiful gold horse's head has vanished, as has my old laundress, who used to call me "Monsieur Vite," though I was anything but quick to pick up her exorbitantly expensive if impeccably turned-out loads of wash. More and more the island is filling up with tearooms and novelty stores for the tourists spilling over from Notre-Dame.

On the way back through the place du Châtelet, my thoughts are often invaded by ghosts—of all those prisoners who were boiled or drawn and quartered here and of all those hogs and geese that were slaughtered around the Tour St.-Jacques. For the original Châtelet was a prison fortress where confessions were wrested from people through torture, where the grisliest executions took place and the cadavers were laid out in full public view. Just next door, the Church of St.-Jacques was called St.-Jacques de la Boucherie and was surrounded by slaughterhouses and butchers' shops. Now everything is bland and antiseptic and the only squeal is of taxi wheels, the only liquid flowing is water in the curious, early-nineteenth-century fountain of sphinxes beneath a gilt Victory tottering on top of a column, the only slaughter is that committed by critics on singers and dancers when they perform badly at one of the two massive theaters put up during the Second Empire. In the Théâtre Musical de Paris, the Ballets Russes had their start in 1909. Whenever I look at the boxes (which the French call *corbeilles*, or "baskets"), I think how Diaghilev on the opening night gave free tickets for those seats to the most beautiful women in town and provided each with an identical showy bouquet. Like all true impresarios he controlled every detail and never failed to produce a *coup de théâtre*.

My one indirect contact with Diaghilev was through

his last secretary, Boris Kochno, who was a young man when he worked for Diaghilev and in his nineties when I met him. I had called him, hoping to interview him about Jean Genet, whom he'd known in the 1940s, when Kochno's lover, Christian Bérard, designed the sets for Genet's play *The Maids*. With his Boris Karloff accent, Kochno had said, "You must understand, Mr. White, that at my age one has no desire to meet new people. I never go out. I live with my memories."

Now, if there was one thing I'd learned in Paris, it was that the cry of every genuine socialite is "I never go out," or "I prefer a good book to an evening of empty *mondanités*," or "If I see anyone, it's just two or three friends, always the same, my life couldn't be duller." These are the very people one sees at a masked ball for cancer at the Palais Garnier or at a charity benefit at the Petit Trianon or at a huge sit-down dinner for three hundred to launch Diane Von Furstenburg's perfume, Tatiana.

So with Kochno, I knew it was just a question of finding which people made up his milieu, because he'd even tripped up and admitted, "Nothing is more important, Mr. White, than one's milieu. When one is young, one prizes only intimacy, especially love. But when one is old, one treasures one's circle more than its individual members."

My friends James Lord (biographer of Giacometti)

and Bernard Minoret (playwright and man-about-town) turned out to be part of Kochno's milieu. They invited me to dinner with him and piled him with questions about Genet all evening. He told us many amusing anecdotes, some of which ended up in my biography, but at one point someone mentioned Picasso. Kochno, with all his macabre, Slavic charm, said, "It's as clear as though it happened yesterday. It must have been in the mid-1920s and I was lunching at the Rond-Point des Champs-Élysées with Picasso, Diaghilev and Stravinsky. Picasso was the first to leave, and as he crossed the street Diaghilev said, 'Take a good look at him. It's as though you were seeing Michelangelo in the streets of Florence.' "

Once, soon after I met Hubert, I went with him to hear Alban Berg's *Wozzeck* at the Châtelet. About twelve rows ahead of us was my American friend Gregory Rowe, a guy who's been in France just ten years but who speaks the language so well he has to show his American passport to prove he's not French. His gestures, his shrugs, his opinions—everything is *pur sang* French, except his enthusiasm, the last boisterous genetic trait to remain in any native American.

Although Hubert must have been initially attracted to my irrepressible urge to help foreigners out when they're wrestling with a map on a windy street corner or to invite every stray in town to Thanksgiving dinner, no matter how ill sorted, or to scream out Gregory's name across the subdued, murmuring stalls, he was quickly embarrassed by it, in accordance with the law that we are always attracted by opposites and then try to turn them into twins (if we don't succeed we're constantly angry, and if we do we lose interest and find a new partner, even more outrageously unsuitable). I don't mean to exaggerate, but this time Hubert sensed I was about to overflow with a truly alarming "Gregory!!" He glared and whispered, "*Du calme, du calme.*" Slowly I subsided. When Hubert saw the look of misery on my face he laughed and said compassionately, "*Pauvre petit . . .*"

Across the street from the Châtelet theater is the Théâtre de la Ville, which was once called the Théâtre Sarah Bernhardt because the tragic actress had taken a fifteen-year lease on the hall in 1899, where she created some of her greatest roles; here, as an old, one-legged woman, she played Napoleon's teenage son in Edmond Rostand's *L'Aiglon*. Her last performance was in *Athalie* in 1920. She was carried onstage in a litter supported by six slaves. The Nazis changed the name of the theater because Bernhardt was Jewish; I think it's scandalous the name has never been changed back. Only the name of the corner bar attests to the identity of the incomparable *tragédienne*. Today the theater is a showcase for modern dance. Here I've seen Merce Cunningham

twitch and gesticulate and Lucinda Childs walk monot- onously in place. When things become too tediously experimental I remind myself that the mad nineteenth- century poet Gérard de Nerval (the only past master whose talent intimidated Genet) hanged himself in front of his hotel on January 26, 1855, his feet dangling just two inches above the ground—precisely where the prompter's box would be located now if there were need of a prompter. Nerval was discovered with his hat still on his head.

CHAPTER XI

Hubert found our apartment through an adver-
tisement in the newspaper *Libération*—one
hundred fifteen square meters with lots of
light pouring in through sixteen windows on
three sides, very centrally located, with a wonderfully
kind and helpful concierge downstairs, and all at a rea-
sonable price. The landlord seemed eager to move us
right in, didn't even ask for references, and made no
objection to a basset hound.

We soon found out why. There was not one but *two*
major building sites just outside our windows and neither was about to be finished "in a few weeks," as our
landlord had airily promised.

Of course, we could have been a bit more observant and noticed that the entire neighborhood was up in arms. In order to construct a six-story underground parking lot the promoters had had to uproot the hundred-year-old chestnut and plane trees. Our concierge, Madame Denise, had joined with the other neighbors in what could be called a "die-in." They linked arms to block the bulldozer's path, to no avail. Once the trees were uprooted, the neighbors put up a white cross in each hole to mark the site of the outrage.

The neighborhood was equally indignant that so little time had been given to the archaeologists, who were naturally curious to see what lay under this most ancient of Roman roads. The hand-painted cloth banners hanging from every balcony proclaimed the site to be a *trou de mémoire*—a pun referring to both a "memory lapse" and a "hole" dug into history. Another banner said that Paris should be made the sister city to "Swiss Cheese Town."

If I'm ever tempted to sleep in on a rainy day, I'm quickly set straight by the clanging and banging, and the groans of cranes and bulldozers, and the workmen's shouts. They're not only excavating the parking lot but also gutting the corner building, which will soon be a Marks & Spencer. The French are frightfully impressed by Marks & Spencer, which they see as the very emblem of British chic instead of just another good place to buy underwear.

The neighborhood was somewhat reconciled to the parking lot when the workers reached the bottom of their dig and gave a giant party to celebrate. Since most of them are Moroccans they roasted several entire lambs on spits. Everyone in the neighborhood was invited and the party went on till dawn.

Somehow the festive mood lingered on, and one afternoon, after a bibulous lunch, an operator let the crane get out of control. It collided with our building and knocked off the cornice under a window just beneath ours.

CHAPTER XII

I often write at the Café Beaubourg, which strikes the English, who love crowded, smoky pubs, as disagreeably austere and new, but which I find airy and calm although there's always something to see. It was built at the end of the 1980s, right across from the Centre Georges Pompidou and the giant digital clock that counts down the *seconds* that remain until the end of the century. At the corner is the always busy fountain designed by Niki de Saint-Phalle and her husband, Jean Tinguely, with a pair of red lips, water squirting from the tits of one of Niki's famous fat ladies, or *nanas*, a top hat that spins, a treble clef in black metal, and so on, all bobbling and twirling—and soaking passersby on

windy days. Fred likes to walk by here because I encourage him to defecate on the grill above the underground center for experimental music, directed by Pierre Boulez, who once refused to give me an interview.

All the waiters at the Café Beaubourg know Fred and automatically serve him a croissant in the morning and a bowl of water on a hot day. Despite an inherent discretion, they will sometimes point out the famous people, most of them Spanish city planners whose names mean nothing to me, but once the waiters intrigued Hubert and me by saying that a psychiatrist sees his patients here. We kept edging our way around, from one table to another; once we were sure we'd found the right man when we heard a woman excitedly telling him she'd symbolically castrated her father. But more and more people say that sort of thing over lunch, so we couldn't be sure. In casing the balcony we learned that the tabletops were all painted by celebrated French artists but not signed lest they be stolen.

One of the liveliest conversationalists I know is Edgardo Cosarinsky, a filmmaker and writer (*Urban Voodoo*) born in Buenos Aires to Russian Jewish parents. He's making a movie now about the handful of Moroccan Jews who stayed on in Tangier after independence in the 1950s and the nearly simultaneous Jewish emigration to the newly founded state of Israel.

He has fascinating tales to tell, about his visit to a Jewish club in the European quarter of Tangier (average age of members: eighty-two) or to a dry goods store, open for only one hour a day, where no new items have been ordered since the 1950s. The stationery sets are browning, the sport shirts, complete with embroidered geometric designs, are irregularly bleached by the sun, and the stacks of towels smell of mildew and mouse shit. Edgardo has a fiendish appetite for this sort of detail.

His favorite theory is that Paris has not changed at all since Balzac's day. For instance, he pointed out a waiter and said, "He was a peasant in the Auvergne just a year ago. His uncle said to his mother, a widow, 'Listen, Pierre is not strong enough to be a peasant.' 'Then he should be a hairdresser,' his mother replied without a pause, 'and I have the address of a beauty school in Lyon.' 'No, I have a better idea,' replied the uncle. 'I know a headwaiter in Paris who will hire him as a busboy.' Now it's a year later and Pierre's already a waiter and talks about Almodóvar films and has his *gourmette* [a gold bracelet] and will be spending his holidays with *un monsieur très bien* in Monaco this August. It's all out of Balzac—Pierre is Lucien de Rubempré and the *monsieur* is Vautrin."

Not long ago I started going to a gay shrink from San Francisco who deals with depression accompanying HIV. He is helping me cope with Hubert's illness. He told me that he'd been touched personally by AIDS. "Oh," I said, "did your lover die?" "Yes," he said, "and both my parents. I was raised by two gay men."

Yesterday I saw him at the Café Beaubourg, listening to and nodding with another balding blond man who was also thirty-something. The Beaubourg shrink! I thought, as one might exclaim, "The Phantom of the Opera," except my friend Christine now claims she once met the real Freud Citron, the true Lacan Express, at the house of our friend Patricia, and she is sure he was one hundred percent French.

CHAPTER XIII

I n the rue des Lombards, just below the windows of my study, seven or eight very old, matronly prostitutes work in shifts. According to Madame Denise, they don't live here but have rented an . . . *atelier*, strictly for work purposes, between the Japanese and Chinese restaurants and across from the sex shop. Between customers they often amble into the local bar, downstairs, Les Piétons, where Madame Denise likes to drink her glass of white wine of an afternoon.

Two of the prostitutes wear mink coats and sweep their white hair up into chignons off the neck. In Paris, it's true, the only women who wear minks are Italian tourists and local prostitutes, but the Italians usually carry a cellular telephone as well, so there's generally no confusion (*"Ciao, Mamma, siamo a Parigi!"*). Another local prostitute, also in her sixties, wears a shiny rubber dress and matching cape, as well as scary, lickable boots. Since God made lots of male masochists and very few female sadists, a prostitute who's willing to be a *dominatrice* can continue her career well into her golden years. No sex could be safer than making Monsieur Micheton dress up in frilly lace panties and dust the atelier while treated to a shower of insults and a taste of the whip. As Madame Denise confides in a whisper, "She can even sit down in an armchair and relax, poor thing."

One of the snowy-haired matrons, still according to Madame Denise, lives in a distant neighborhood with her grown son, a proud and respectable *garçon de café*. Over the decades she has told him she works at the Les Halles branch of the giant bookstore FNAC, and he has never doubted her story.

One of the prostitutes is slightly younger, wears a gray ankle-length coat overprinted with the Hapsburgs' double eagle, and has a yappy dog named Mickey. Ceaseless dog-walking is a good reason to live in the streets, and two of the other women have dogs, too— always tiny, beribboned puppies, I've remarked, as though an obese aging dog would invite unwelcome comparisons.

During the day three or four of the women stand in their doorway and gossip with one another and scold their puppies. They seldom seem troubled by clients as they clobber stiffly down the stretch of cobbled street in their high heels. It crosses my mind that prostitution is just an innocent excuse for hanging out and chewing the fat with the girls. At night, however, young men in search of maternal love do stand in the street, even under the rain, looking longingly up to the atelier.

One afternoon I saw a respectable young mother in a pleated navy blue skirt hurry past with her daughter. She was aghast when the whores started waving in their grandmotherly way to the little girl and the child went running toward Mickey and all that shiny rubber, so much prettier than a twin set and pearls.

CHAPTER XIV

The grocery just on the other side of the rue St.-Martin is a mom-and-pop store run by a Cambodian man and his wife and daughter. Outside there's a slightly discouraged-looking fruit and vegetable stand under an awning. The doorway is covered with labels, hundreds and hundreds of them, that have come off oranges and bananas—the only sign that a poet works here.

The job can't be easy, since so many of the customers are drunks who come staggering in demanding a bottle of red wine. The hours are long, and the doors always open when it's cold outside; the checkout and cash register are right next to the entrance. There are many shoplifters as well.

But the owner and his family are invariably kind and patient and smiling. One day I noticed a snapshot of the owner above the cash register, tucked into the spice rack, next to the saffron. In the photograph he was dressed in a tuxedo and was shaking the hand of a white man dressed similarly.

When I asked the owner about the event, he explained, blushing in that total, harvest-moon way that Asian men have, that he'd received an award from someone in the Ministry of Culture as the best Cambodian poet writing in France. He told me that he wrote short quatrains, often about nature. No wonder, I thought, looking out the door at the rain-slick cobbles, the only trees in the neighborhood bulldozed to make way for the parking lot.

He showed me his notepad for writing out receipts for customers. On each facing page he has a place for jotting down lines of poetry as they come winging their way to him. When no customers come into the shop for a half-hour or more during the dog days of August, he can sometimes work out an entire stanza. Four of his poems recently were broadcast on the radio.

I told him I was a writer, too, though nothing so grand as a poet. I could appreciate his kind of poetry, I said, since I'd majored in classical Chinese at my university and I'd been especially attracted to the T'ang poets Tu Fu and Li Po.

Actually, I was greatly exaggerating my erudition, since I had been a very lazy student, undisciplined and depressed, and my Chinese professor would even phone me from class to get me out of bed in the morning. I usually caught only the last half-hour of language practice. I did make thousands of flash cards with the Chinese character on one side and on the other the pronunciation and meaning—or rather meanings, since Chinese, as the oldest continuous written language still in use, has accumulated dozens of meanings for each character over the centuries. As a student I excused my lack of conversational fluency by saying I was interested only in classical Chinese; no more than three other people on my campus could detect my incompetence in the written language. When I graduated I received a degree with honors in Chinese, despite the fact that I couldn't read, write or speak the language. I had intended to go on to Harvard to obtain a doctorate, an accomplishment that would lead to a nice sinecure in Sinology somewhere and give me plenty of time to write fiction—a fine plan, but one I never put into practice since I fell in love with someone at my university and followed him to New York. There I became a journalist and five years later I threw out ten boxes of Chinese flash cards.

The grocer's daughter is studying Chinese, and she and her father always greet me with handshakes and smiles and even bows, as though I must be very scholarly indeed. Only the mother seems to have sized me up as the fraud I am. Now each visit to the grocery, which I used to dash into and out of unshaved, sockless in loafers, my hair standing on end, has taken on the dimensions of a state ceremony. I remember that at a traditional Chinese dinner the guest could always fill a lull by exclaiming that the meal was far too luxurious for him, to which the host would reply (I think), "*Bu tsai!*" which means (I think), "There aren't even any vegetables." I used to think such purely formulaic exchanges must be wonderfully restful. Now I realize that even formulas can breed anxiety, though of a reassuring and unvarying kind; the nervousness is simply performance anxiety, known the world over to actors, Don Juans and cultural frauds.

Fred's best friend in the neighborhood is Bol de Riz (Rice Bowl)—a hateful nickname, the only one I know, for a lovable Vietnamese eccentric who lives in the streets. He calls me "Papi," which I'm too vain to like; perhaps he's referring to my gray hair, or to my paternal role with my "child," Fred. At least I've been spared the even more disagreeable "Pépère" (Gramps).

Bol de Riz's own age is mysterious, although he once told me we were the same age.

People in the neighborhood, especially the guys who sell old clothes and furs across from the Church of St.-Merri, must give him things to wear. He has an extraordinary fashion sense and will often come up with combinations worthy of Comme des Garçons. One winter day I saw him in a black tricorne over black earmuffs, an Yves Klein blue fake-fur coat belted with a hemp rope, mountain climber's boots with untied red laces, and high striped wool stockings pulled up over his trouser legs.

Every morning at six he swabs out the corner restaurant for just twenty francs and lustily sings elaborate songs of his own devising that are as talky and unmelodic as Joni Mitchell's or (in France) Barbara's. When he's finished his work he often continues serenading our windows, so caught up is he in the twists and turns of his highly plotted lyrics.

He runs errands for everyone in the neighborhood—he'll go to the bank to get rolls of coins for the newspapers kiosk, or carry people's groceries, or lure customers into the Quimper pottery store by making elaborate flourishing bows to passing tourists (this strategy, alas, usually scares them off). Wherever he goes he's dressed in his extraordinary outfits, which give him the look of a Sherpa guide and a freaky, post-punk runway model.

Once every two weeks he becomes blind drunk. His

face turns red, his eyes fill with blood, his mouth hangs open, his breath wheezes forth rancid fumes, and he stands stock-still in the middle of the street, wherever chance and the one neuron that is still dimly blinking have led him.

On sober days when he sees Fred he cries, "*Mon bébé*," and rolls on the ground with Fred in his arms. He licks Fred's face and kisses his belly, especially where the pink shows through on the spot where Fred's fur has been rubbed off from mounting the stairs to our apartment. At first Fred was distrustful of so much exuberance. I think he was afraid Bol de Riz might somehow hurt him; maybe he mistook his cries of joy for anger. But now Fred is used to him and starts galloping toward him the minute he sees him. Such mutual displays of puppy love delight Fred, but when they come to an end he shakes his long ears from side to side as though awakening from a childish dream. On the way home Fred is unusually subdued, hoping to suggest he was playing merely to indulge poor, darling, demented Bol. If we leave the windows open on a warm morning when Bol de Riz is singing, Fred starts to whimper to go out and join him.

Once a month the café and tobacco store across from the church is open. It's owned by a very feeble old lady. The café is piled high with boxes, and only a narrow path between them leads to the bar. One naked bulb

provides the only light. Six months ago the lady was knocked down and robbed by local ruffians, and now she almost never opens her store. People say she's a fabulously rich miser and owns half of the buildings in the neighborhood, but that's the sort of thing people always say about a poor old lady they'd otherwise have to feel bad about and even help.

The Church of St.-Merri is usually surrounded by tramps—not aggressive, noisy ones like those in New York, but calm, polite beggars who usually do nothing more alarming than extend a hand and say, "*Une petite pièce, m'sieurs-dames!*" They're always the same tramps, known to everyone, neighborhood fixtures. During severe cold spells the church will open up a free soup kitchen for all the destitute. Often tramps gather inside to keep warm, but the church is almost never heated. For vespers its double doors are thrown open, its altar candles are lit, a spotlight is directed toward a gloria of the Holy Spirit contained in a burst of golden stucco sun rays, and an organist, unseen, laborious, fills the street with the ceaseless musical yardgoods of a Fauré fantasia.

The original Saint Merri (or Médéric) lived in a small chapel on this very site, where he was buried on August 29, in the year 700. His relics worked wonders, and when they were exhumed to be placed in a sumptuous casket they shone like jewels—which so impressed a rich bystander, Eudes the Falconer, that he built a fine church to house the relics. In 1520 the parish had become so prosperous and crowded with merchants that they decided to build a newer, bigger church in an already rather old-fashioned style, Flamboyant Gothic. This was the church that was badly damaged during the Revolution; the building was turned into a saltpeter factory, then handed over, from 1797 to 1801, to a group of deist merchants, the Théophilanthropes, who renamed it the Temple of Commerce. When the building became a church again after the Restoration, the façade had to be entirely restored. The Catholic satanist Huysmans, author of the decadent novel *Against the Grain*, was especially fond of the statues of a hare and a dog above the right door. Perhaps because of these friendly symbols, Fred always wants to enter the church. I invariably remind him he can't, since, unlike us, he doesn't have an immortal soul. That's a remark bound to infuriate Hubert, who's from a long line of militant atheists: "If anyone I know has a soul, it's Fred. Just look at his warm, innocent eyes. Really, Edmund, how can you say something so blasphemous?"

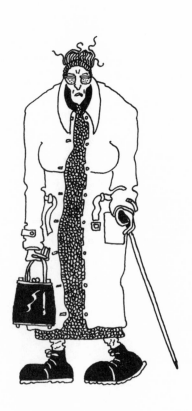

CHAPTER XV

One August evening I was having dinner at our place with Peter Kurth, the American biographer. We were comparing notes about all the difficulties in researching the biography of people like Jean Genet or Peter's current subject, Isadora Duncan, people who turned their own lives into myths and had a creative approach to the truth.

Peter was on his way back from Russia, where he'd been investigating Isadora's relationship to Esenin, the flamboyant bisexual poet. The next day he'd be heading home to the States. He was discouraged by the sinking level of culture throughout the world. "No one even knows who Isadora was anymore," he said gloomily.

"Oh, surely," I said, "they've all heard about the American modern dancer who danced barefoot and nude for the Bolsheviks or who was kept by Singer of the sewing machine or who strangled herself when her scarf was caught in the wire wheels of a roadster."

"Not really," he said. He looked belligerently at Fred, who was sleeping on his back with all four paws in the air though folded back gracefully. "God, is that dog fat!" he said.

"He is not. The winner of the Westminster Dog Show this year was a basset and he was much more jowly."

But Peter was determined to lash out at a being so infernally relaxed as Fred, even inert, unaware of a biographer's many worries. "And how banal to name him Fred the Basset."

"We didn't even know about that comic-strip character," I protested. "We named him after a French psychiatrist friend, Frédéric."

Fred's right front paw twitched insouciantly with a ghostly Pavlovian response to the mention of his name.

Just then a young woman's voice, penetrating and perfectly pitched, free of all accompaniment, rang out in the old streets below. We went to the open window and watched her, barefoot, shiny hair streaming down her back, as she belted out one show tune after another in English. Her voice was strong and clear and not to be confused with anyone else's. The diners sitting under the awning on the curb didn't appear to appreciate her, perhaps because they'd just been dazzled by three tap dancers dressed up as ducks, a tough act to follow.

Peter and I, however, adored her voice and called out to her to wait for us to come down to the street. She nodded, looking somewhat confused.

When we joined her, with Fred, we invited her to the Café Beaubourg. She told us her whole story—how she'd come from Australia and was now studying song and dance. "I'm determined," she said, "to become the new Isadora!"

CHAPTER XVI

We read a book by Mario Praz, an Italian critic, in which he describes all the objects in his palatial apartment in Rome, giving their pedigree and provenance and all his personal associations, including sometimes quite shocking revelations about his unhappy marriage and estranged daughter. Hubert and I keep thinking it would be funny to do a sort of comic version about our own apartment and all our junk, but I'm sometimes worried he won't have enough time left to do the pictures.

I say "junk," but Hubert would bridle at such a word. To him our place is a treasure house where we store up all the marvels we've unearthed on our trips. Or rather, *his* marvels, since his finds are all discoveries of museum-level artifacts, whereas poor old gullible Ed gets taken to the cleaner's every time.

Take the misshapen little jug with its elephant-gray hide and mold-blue inner glaze, the pure product of an arts-and-crafts class taught in an asylum by an incompetent to an indifferent on Thorazine, a three-dimensional daub Hubert seized on in what used to be East Berlin at a street fair across the canal from the Pergamon Museum. "It's obviously a . . . yes, a *honey pourer* from the late eighteenth century. I've *studied* such objects in paintings of the period. Laugh all you like, you'll see, an expert will come here one day and offer us a fabulous sum for it." He grows quiet and, irked, adds, "Funny that you can't see it. Usually your taste is rather good."

On the same trip Hubert bought me a Russian icon being hawked by a gentle young Slav. Hubert rejected other lacquered, highly colored icons in favor of this one, which has a warped wood back and a tin cover snipped into small openings to reveal paintings of Christ, his mother and various angels, all hopelessly rotted away or blackened with candle smoke except for one ineffaceable angel on the left with a consoling little salutation unscrolling from its mouth like ticker tape.

Hubert was racked with remorse for nights after this purchase; he thought he'd virtually stolen this masterpiece out of an impoverished Russian home of fallen aristocrats.

In a Toronto shop (which the French would say was run by a *brocanteur*, to mark a midway point between the noble antique dealer and the ignominious junkman), Hubert bought a 1930s lamp, now in his bedroom, with a chrome tango dancer dipping beside a clouded glass column—an obvious Original, which the pitifully unsuspecting dealer had let slip out of his careless hands for mere pennies. Curiously, the same shopkeeper became a cynical exploiter of a shockingly naïve American when he sold me, at an exorbitant price, a green bowl of 1950s Finnish art glass (now filled with walnuts in the sitting room)—a worthless and ugly folly that Hubert keeps hiding away in the kitchen to spare me further embarrassment.

Hubert has a shelf of horrors he loves to show squeamish guests—a scorpion under glass, a tarantula in a paperweight, a Chinese portable cage in which to carry crickets (presently empty), and best of all, an immense ostrich foot outfitted with a very nasty-looking claw—which resembles a lethal homemade weapon cobbled together by a Road Warrior.

Showing the foot always provides Hubert with an opportunity to discuss his two years in Ethiopia. On our sitting room walls we have two large paintings, as impressive as they are grim, which Hubert bought in

Addis Ababa, where he taught architecture for the French government. One painting depicts a squadron of men in blue-and-green uniforms marching and waving huge red banners. The other shows three military dictators in army uniform on a podium. They are staring directly at us while their followers, all identical men, avert their eyes either to the right or to the left. As Hubert explains, these canvases were done by a man who'd been one of Haile Selassie's official painters, but after the emperor was replaced by communists the artist gave up royal jousts and lions as his subjects and turned to dispiriting Marxist parades. Hubert met the painter, bought his work and took his picture. In the photo he's shown in front of one of his paintings, but the African sunlight is so bright that the canvas is bleached white; only where his shadow falls across it are the colors and shapes visible.

Ethiopia remains such a reference for Hubert that he compares almost everything with it. When he went to New York for the first time he surprised me by comparing Manhattan to Addis Ababa. I was even more confused when he thought the New Mexico landscape looked like that of Ethiopia. Whenever Hubert's in a cross mood, our friend Christine (who lived with us in the States for a year) can get him out of it by diplomatically asking him a question about Ethiopia.

Nothing about that exotic, hermetic country seems

excessive to Hubert or his ex-wife, Fabienne. She's an expert in Ethiopian culture and speaks three of the country's languages. She once showed me a photo of a strangely *hairy* arch of triumph. As she explained, since Mussolini's invading troops kept building Roman arches to celebrate their Abyssinian victories, the Ethiopian army decided after a victory of their own to put up an arch to which they tacked the severed testicles of their Italian prisoners. A photo (*this* photo) was duly sent to Mussolini. Hubert keeps wangling for a Xerox of it to add to his shelf of horrors, to be placed next to the ostrich foot.

If Hubert is guilty of exaggerating the importance of his purchases, I'm not above my own fudging. An orange-and-black lacquered coffee table in the sitting room comes from Chicago, so I've somehow decided to attribute it to Marx, a famous midwestern designer of the 1940s, though I have nothing but wishing to substantiate my claim; in a similar spirit of optimism I've assigned the green-and-gold wrought-iron French end table to Poillerat, though my only basis for such an attribution is a near likeness I once came across in a photo book about 1940s furniture designers.

Hubert's brother has dubbed the bedroom the "White Museum" since Hubert has put up dozens of photos of me, everything from the two Mapplethorpe portraits (one screaming), taken in 1981, when I was still thin, to a more recent double portrait by Arthur Patten of Fred and me, each of us sporting three chins. I'm so embarrassed by the Musée White that I call it "Hubert's Room" and pray he won't say it's ours.

Although Hubert gets skinnier and skinnier, he likes it that Fred and I remain so robust. Sometimes, however, when I'm too hardheaded, he'll say, "You're just like Fred"—a reference to the basset's notoriously single-minded character. But since he loves Fred so much, I can't take the reproach as a genuine insult.

When I look around our "House of Life" (the title of Mario Praz's book), I feel a bit apprehensive. Hubert has said from the beginning that he's decorating it for me so I'll have a place to live after he's gone, though I can scarcely imagine rattling around it alone.

Afterword

SO MANY of my friends with AIDS have wanted to write a book or make some other kind of work of art to celebrate or at least to mark their passage on earth and in time. Few of these ambitions have been realized, either because illness has interfered with their execution or because the world (or the marketplace) has taken no interest in their efforts.

Hubert Sorin, my lover, who died just two hours ago in the Polyclinique du Sud in Marrakesh, was an architect who turned himself into an illustrator with a remarkable patience and diligence and above all with a flair for capitalizing on his talents and pictorial discoveries.

He was a meticulous, orderly young man (he was just

thirty-two years old) with a clear, blue-gray eye for detail and for visual (and literary) quality. When he realized in 1990 that he could no longer work as an architect, with simplicity and professionalism he set about becoming an artist.

Like many men and women of his generation in France, he took a vivid pleasure in adult comic books and was always picking up the latest *Fluide glacial* or a reprint of a classic *Astérix* or *Tintin*. Although he'd long entertained vague thoughts about becoming a painter, he was well informed enough to know that the art world has little to do with art and quite a bit to do with trends that are both commercial and pretentiously art-historical. He realized he'd have much more freedom if he took up the so-called secondary art of illustration.

In 1990, when we were living in the United States, he started to acquire his characteristic line, his *patte*, through hundreds of hours of drawing cartoon figures. They were seldom elaborate—in the beginning they were just a dash and a knot, a stick and a ball, a ponytail and glasses: a rapid jet of lovely calligraphy.

And from the first these little people, *ces bonhommes et bonnes femmes*, were integers in a storytelling calculus of his own devising. He *saw stories* and, as with the ancient Egyptian scribes, his columns and columns of figures and animals were intrinsically narrative. He'd satirize himself as the acid-tongued Frenchman among well-meaning American hicks. Or he'd imagine the Chinese couple who cleaned for us once a week as spies sending back to their government a confused, hilarious report on our peculiar activities. The amorous adventures of our friends were also subjects for his sharp if affectionate eye. Of course his great theme was cultural differences.

I'm writing this page with his beautiful Art Pen, which he always forbade me to touch; today I couldn't find anything else to write with, and I wanted to—needed to—give a form to my grief that he would have approved of. That's why I'm daring to use your pen, Hubert. Four days before he died he said that after his death I should write something about him for our book—"Not to praise me," he was careful to add, "but just for the sake of the book."

He put together two books, this one and an earlier one. The first, *Mémoires dessinées*, was published in Paris in 1992 as a limited-edition artist's book by Rachel Stella, the art dealer and daughter of painter Frank Stella and art critic Barbara Rose. Rachel was convinced of Hubert's importance as an artist and celebrated the publication of his book with a big, glamorous party in her gallery, an evening attended by many French and American collectors, writers and figures in the art world.

Mémoires dessinées is a quirky, droll, sometimes bitchy look at the people he and I were meeting in France and the States. The chapters are "comic strips," that is, successive frames of images and words telling a story, though the term "comic strip" seems misleading. The stories are all about the foibles and eccentricities of members of our circle, whom Hubert invariably saw in mythic terms. He assumed readers would recognize the names of our friends; perhaps now they'll arrange for their names of become household words just to substantiate this generous whim of his.

The figures, no longer his *petits bonhommes*, were now drawn with a hieratic sophistication, as though Aubrey Beardsley had gone pharaonic. The words, which switched blithely in mid-sentence from English to French, revealed a sensitivity to social nuance which reminds us that in French *malicieux* means "sly" and *malin* means "clever"; the evil, or *mal*, in each word is the necessary spice for the savory dish. Hubert's expectations of his readers were absurdly demanding—but no higher than those of most contemporary poets, I suppose.

He always wanted us to work on a book together, but I've never liked collaborations. Nor did I think I could find a tone that would go with his drawings (the word he liked, *dessins*, as opposed to "illustrations"). As his health began to deteriorate rapidly after we moved in

January 1993 to the Châtelet district of Paris, I overcame my misgivings and laziness, and a few months later we started to work on *Our Paris*. He was determined to finish the book before he died; unlike me, he seemed to know he had only a very limited time to live—a year and six weeks, to be exact.

I kept thinking he'd live on and on. I'd been diagnosed as HIV positive in 1985 and my health had in no way deteriorated. Hubert was receiving two different experimental treatments, one of which seemed promising. I suppose I let myself be seduced by the current cant about AIDS becoming a manageable chronic disease like diabetes. It's no such thing, but I was encouraged to hold on to this fantasy by my love for him and my fear of losing him. He knew the truth, though, and in his last three months longed to die in order to be freed of an existence that had become almost entirely one of suffering.

What kept him alive was the idea of finishing this book. At first he worked far ahead of me, although in the last two months I caught up with him. Sometimes he had only a good half-hour a day, but that half-hour he devoted to drawing. He did the cover and I completed all the texts just before we set off on a last trip to Morocco. Even there he hoped to work and brought along his Art Pen and Canson paper. He wanted to do one last drawing (of the young Australian woman singing in the streets), to appear at the very end in order to balance the first drawing of the street singer.

He died in Marrakesh at dawn on March 17, 1994, the very day on which I'm writing this afterword. He had wanted to see the desert. As an architecture student he had specialized in the construction of the Muslim *hammam* and had drawn historic buildings in Fez. This interest, as well as memories of an early visit to the desert in Tunisia, attracted him to southern Morocco. On the last full day of his life we traveled by automobile from Erfoud, in the Sahara, to Ouarzazate, passing through one oasis after another. It was the end of Ramadan, and the men were dressed in festive white, the women in black and black sequins, woven red belts around their waists. He saw a camel grazing at liberty. We went through entire towns of shaped and incised earth mixed with straw and cement or chalk. Hubert kept murmuring, "*Superbe, c'est superbe. . . .*"

Hubert had been the one to choose our apartment. He'd always detested (quite irrationally, I thought) what he called the "petit bourgeois" atmosphere of the place Maubert in the Fifth Arrondissement, our previous, calmer, more residential address. And he immediately took to our new neighborhood of hookers, tramps, tourists, artists, shoppers and colorful local characters. He loved our concierge with her sweetness and warmhearted if utterly disabused acceptance of all the walking wounded in the *quartier*. He specially loved her *loge*, her little apartment-cum-office, with the lace curtains, real flowers and fake flowers, the cooking smells, the dismal blue-green paint, the table that served as distribution point for the mail in the morning, ironing board in the afternoon, kitchen counter in the evening (a convenient place to prepare avocado halves stuffed with shrimp in mayonnaise). She knew he was seriously ill, and she once told me, forefinger to her lips, refusing to name his disease, that I could count on her to shop and even cook for us—purest folly, since because of her own faltering health she could scarcely walk. That Hubert chose to show her dancing is a tribute to her spiritual gaiety—and his.

He was brave. In the first two years of his illness he had a grumbling French frankness about every ache and pain; never was an upper lip less stiff. For the last two years, despite excruciating and almost constant pain, he never complained at all. Nor did he ever talk about his fear of dying (if he was in fact afraid) or his speculations about ultimate meanings. He was an atheist and on his mother's side belonged to a third generation of convinced nonbelievers. He did enjoy, in a melancholy, aesthetic way, his almost daily visits to St.-Merri or St.-Eustache; our friend Father Riches represented a Firbankian blend of camp, piety and goodness that spoke directly to Hubert's soul.

What mattered to Hubert were art and love: like Tosca he could have declared, "*Vissi d'arte, vissi d'amore*." He was alarmingly quick to excommunicate friends, he was indifferent to the ebb and flow of politics, he had a seigneurial disregard for money. He was delighted by gossip and by anecdotes that illuminate character, and as he became increasingly housebound he relied on me to bring bits of tinsel back to the nest. He had put together a highly personal *art de vivre* over the years and had come to prize good food and good wine, the expressive and sensational resources of sex, an unacademic and proudly subjective response to painting and literature, a detached connoisseur's fascination with human oddities. In the last two years he could scarcely eat (he suffered terribly from chronic pancreatitis), he no longer drank, and he lost his appetite for sex. But he remained infatuated with art and with the everyday occurrences that could be shaped by storytelling.

For *Our Paris*, Hubert evolved a more fluid style than his earlier *Yellow Book*—Second Dynasty manner. Now he adopted a technique more sensitive to notations of movement and gesture. I had so much trouble working on my text, largely because I had the superstition (which turned out to be clairvoyance) that if I arrived at the end of our one thousand and one nights he would die, as proved to be the case. He pressed me to hurry and in the end he succeeded in galvanizing me. Like

Scheherazade I would read him each small chapter as I finished it, and he'd make a suggestion or two but seemed happy for the most part, as well he should have been since I'd pitched the book to vibrate to the tautness of his sensibility. Whether it will please anyone else I have no way of knowing (and have scarcely thought about till now). Unlike Scheherazade I'm still alive at the end of the last tale, but my sultan is dead.

The subtitle alludes to Hubert's earlier *Mémoires dess-inées* and to something he once said about his method. I'd suggested he sketch from life or from photos, but he shot back with the speed and clarity of conviction that he worked exclusively from memory and had no inter-est in letting reality sit for him if it was unmediated by his fancy. I don't know where he came up with this idea, but I adapted it as my own, and it contributes to the slightly childlike, perhaps *faux naif*, certainly stylized quality of words and images.

Although we never talked about it, this tone con-joined us to silence about AIDS; it was our undoubtedly absurd notion of gallantry that made us pretend (in his drawings) that his body was not aging and wasting away or (in my chapters) that we had nothing more serious to do than loaf in the streets and give dinner parties. All bluff, since toward the end we seldom saw anyone or went anywhere. Hubert came to despise his emaciated body, but in his drawings he remains as dapper and handsome and *élancé* as he was the day I met him, five years ago.

During the last three months we had to give Fred, our basset hound, to Hubert's brother in Nice because Hubert could no longer go down the five flights and I couldn't take care of both Hubert and Fred; but in our book we remain an eternal trio, our silhouettes against the Tour St.-Jacques. For many homosexual couples (or childless couples in general), dogs are like children. Certainly Fred, whom Hubert had chosen the instant he saw him in a Massachusetts kennel, was our spoiled and impossible baby, who jumped on people, tore their stockings and trousers, made a mess if left alone for more than two hours, destroyed the furniture when he was a puppy—but whom we forgave everything. We slept with him. He was a tender, vigilant, easily awakened nurse during the long hours every day when he and Hubert napped.

Despite the sometimes catty sound of this book, its name-dropping and archness, I hope at least a few readers will recognize that its subtext is love. Hubert loved me with unwavering devotion. Once he'd decided to give up his wife, his job and his country to move to the States with me, he never looked back. I'd invited a young French woman friend of mine to move with us to Providence, Rhode Island, partly to mitigate what I assumed Hubert would feel was the social curse of living openly with another man. Wasted effort, for he was proud to be—and to be seen as—my lover, though he took almost no interest in other homosexuals. In his own eyes he was unique, beyond categories, and for him our love enjoyed the same Olympian dispensation.

I loved him, too, in my cold, stinting, confused way. I wanted to keep him alive as long as possible. This book gave us something to do while waiting for the end. It is exactly the monument Hubert, this determined, dandified young man, wanted and got.

Marrakesh
March 17, 1994

A NOTE ABOUT THE AUTHOR
AND THE ILLUSTRATOR

Edmund White was born in Cincinnati in 1940. He has taught literature and creative writing at Yale, Johns Hopkins, New York University, and Columbia, was a full professor of English at Brown, and served as executive director of the New York Institute for the Humanities. In 1983 he received a Guggenheim fellowship and the award in literature from the American Academy and Institute of Arts and Letters. In 1993 he was made a Chevalier de l'Ordre des Arts et Lettres; he is now an officer of that organization. For his book *Genet: A Biography* (1994), he was awarded the National Book Critics Circle Award and the Lambda Literary Award. His other books include *Forgetting Elena, Nocturnes for the King of Naples, States of Desire:*

Travels in Gay America, A Boy's Own Story, Caracole, The Beautiful Room Is Empty, Skinned Alive, a short biography of Proust, a novel about Paris called *The Married Man*, and *The Flâneur: A Stroll Through the Paradoxes of Paris*. He lived in Paris for sixteen years and now teaches at Princeton and lives in New York.

Hubert Sorin was an architect and illustrator. He was born in 1962 in Nantes, where he received a degree in architecture. He subsequently taught architecture for two years in Addis Ababa. Upon his return to Paris he went to work for Jean-Jacques Ory, who directed at that time the largest architectural office in France. After retiring at the end of 1989, Sorin became an illustrator and did the drawings for *Mémoires dessinées* (for which he also wrote the texts) and *Our Paris*. He died in March 1994 and is buried in Paris at Père-Lachaise.

A NOTE ON THE TYPE

This book was set in Fournier, a typeface named for Pierre Simon Fournier *fils* (1712-1768), a celebrated French type designer. Coming from a family of type-founders, Fournier was an extraordinarily prolific designer of typefaces and of typographic ornaments. He was also the author of the important *Manuel typographique* (1764-1766), in which he attempted to work out a system standardizing type measurement in points, a system that is still in use internationally.

Fournier's type is considered transitional in that it drew its inspiration from the old style, yet was ingeniously innovational, providing for an elegant, legible appearance. In 1925 his type was revived by the Monotype Corporation of London.

Designed and composed by Sarah Maya Gubkin
Printed and bound by Quebecor,
Martinsburg, West Virginia